The
Last
Camel

D0907467

The Last Camel

True Stories of Somalia

Jeanne D'Haem

The Red Sea Press, Inc.
Publishers and Distributors of Third World Books

11-D Princess Rd   **RSP**   P.O. Box 48

Lawrenceville, NJ 08648   Asmara, ERITREA

The Red Sea Press, Inc.
Publishers and Distributors of Third World Books

11-D Princess Rd   P.O. Box 48
Lawrenceville, NJ 08648   Asmara, ERITREA

Book design: Jonathan Gullery
Cover design: Linda Nickens
Book illustrations: Aaron Wilson

Library of Congress Cataloging-in-Publication Data

D'Haem, Jeanne.
        The last camel ; true stories of Somalia / by Jeanne D'Haem.
            p.   cm.
        ISBN 1-56902-040-X (cloth : alk. paper). -- ISBN 1-56902-041-8
(paper : alk. paper)
        1. Arabsiyo (Somalia)–Social life and customs. 2. D'Haem,
Jeanne. 3. Peace Corps–Somalia--Arabsiyo. 4. Arabsiyo (Somalia) -
-Description and travel. I. Title.
DT409.A73D47   1997
967.73--dc21
                                                            97-8108
PRINTED IN CANADA   CIP

This book is dedicated to
Linda Chirchrillo

Contents

Acknowledgements

The author is grateful to the Somali Peace Corps Volunteers who shared the frustrations and the fun of this great adventure and my Somali friends who taught a stranger to understand the desert. Special thanks to Tom Smoyer for the pictures used for the illustrations and to Abby Thomas for her suggestions on the language. My friend, Maureen Needham, my sister, Susan Norman, and my daughter, Jennifer Kobrin, believed in me and encouraged this project.

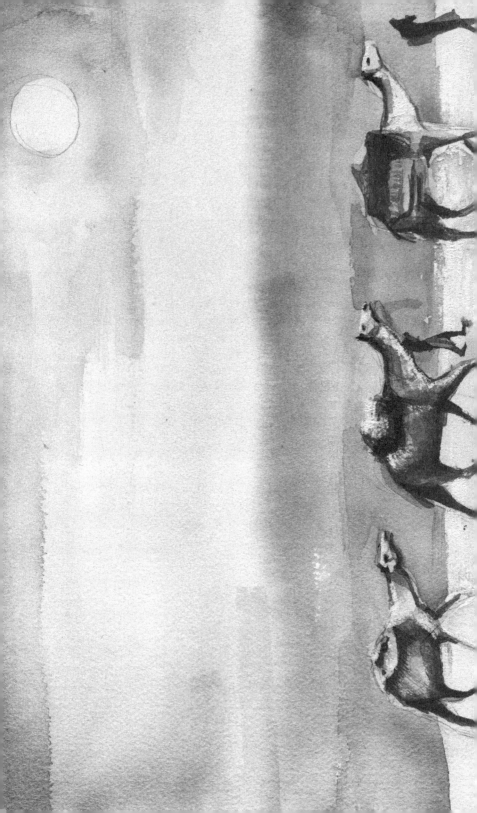

Introduction

At night in Somalia, millions of dazzling stars are held in place by the overturned bowl that is the sky. I can imagine wise men following one of those brilliant beacons. Somaliland is the ancient "Land of Punt" mentioned in the Bible. Legends say that the three wise men who visited the infant Jesus with gifts of gold, frankincense, and myrrh were Puntite kings. Frankincense is a gum resin which gives off a sweet-spicy odor when burned. It is used in medicinal plasters and also symbolizes prayer. It is still burned at the birth of a child in Somalia. Myrrh is also a resin, it comes from the thorny golol (*commiphora abyssinica*) tree. It ranges in color from yellow to brown and is highly prized as an ingredient in perfume and incense. The resin is used as a medicine for inflammations. The gold market in Mogadishu has sold bracelets, earrings, and rings with a definite Arabic influence in design for hundreds of years. The pieces are made of pure 24-karat gold, which has no added alloy.

Sitting outside my little house one night in the village of Arabsiyo, I was stunned to see a brilliant star actually moving across the sky. I wondered excitedly if it was a UFO. Subti, one of the Somali teachers at my school, explained it was the *Hydigi Merican* (the American Star). The nomads tracked the satellites while they watched their flocks of camels and goats by night. Subti could not believe that I had never seen the *Hydigi* sent into the sky by the Americans and the Russians.

You can clearly see the constellation of Cassiopeia in the autumn skies in Arabsiyo. The shore of the Indian Ocean around Somalia was the legendary land of Queen Cassiopeia and King Cepheus. In Roman mythology, Cassiopeia bragged that she was more beautiful than the sea nymphs. They complained to Poseidon who sent Cetus to lay waste the shores of Somalia as punishment. Cassiopeia chained her daughter Andromeda to rocks at the shore as a sacrifice to Cetus, but Perseus flew by on Pegasus and rescued her. Then he turned Cetus to stone with Medusa's head.

I have often felt that Cetus must have destroyed the Somali countryside, it is so rough and barren. Somali women, however, are universally beautiful and I could understand why the sea nymphs were jealous. The men are also physically attractive, but hot-tempered. The best trait of the Somali people—independence and a strong will to survive under any circumstances—has been honed for centuries in the difficult, unforgiving climate. The struggle for water rights is not won by the indecisive or the passive. Ironically, however, these traditional Somali strengths are a weakness as they confront a world in which machine guns have replaced sticks and shouting. Aggressive tendencies ensured survival in the nomadic societies of the past, but these proclivities, tangled with tribal obligations and the infusion of modern weapons, have played a large part in creating the current chaos in that country.

Sir Richard Burton was one of the earliest Europeans to travel among the Somali, and only the equally bold and adventurous have followed. He called his book about those experiences *First Footsteps in East Africa*. In 1882 Sir Richard noted that the natives in Berbera, a Northern port on the Indian Ocean, liked to attract bats to live in their houses. They had noticed that bats eat mosquitoes and do a good job of keeping the insect population down. They had also observed that malarial fever coincided with the mosquito season. Sir Richard dismissed this connection between mosquitoes and malaria as a native superstition, much to the suffering of many in the years before the causal relationship was accepted

Burton has my sympathy, however. It is never easy to understand what it is that you see in Somalia. I often misunderstood what was happening, then made everything worse by insisting on my misguided directives. After all, I joined the Peace Corps to help people. Most Somalis did not consider me helpful at all. When I cried in frustration about this to my friend Asha, she told me, "Listen and watch, listen and watch. When you finally think that you understand, do not say anything, because you don't. You need to listen and watch some more. You cannot speak until you have learned to listen." She pointed to her mother pounding grain in the courtyard of the house and continued, "Somali women no longer wear the black envelope of purdah, but they will always see the world through the veil of their experiences. You cannot communicate with them until you see things as they do." Asha lived in London for many years with her father, who was a Somali diplomat. She understood better than anyone else the discrepancies between the Somali view of the world and mine.

Asha taught me to listen carefully to the stories everyone told and to use them to understand the outer culture and the inner voices of those around me. People describe themselves by the stories they tell about their lives and are defined by their experiences. The knowledge of a person's story or history is an important key to understanding their perspective and the actions they take. I wrote this book as a collection of stories about the people I knew in Arabsiyo because it is the only way I could share my experience of the Somali people I knew. When I lived there, I learned that you must look carefully in order to see the fragile beauty of the desert and the resourceful people who grace the land. If you are not mindful you may not recognize what is there, and you may even upset the delicate system that succeeds in the remorseless desert.

I was a Peace Corps Volunteer in Northern Somalia in 1968. I lost thirty ponds when I lived there. Not because I didn't have money for food (I had plenty by Somali standards), and not because there was no food (there was enough to stay alive). I didn't eat because the meat was covered with flies, the flour was riddled with weevils, and the tinned tuna from China gave me terrible diarrhea. I ate to live, I didn't live to eat. Many of the paradigms basic to our lives in the West are reversed in Somalia.

I won't say that I was a good volunteer. Somalia is not an easy place to live. There were few modern amenities and life was occasionally dangerous, but usually it was very quiet. This lulls one into complacency, and dims the powers of observation. During the long hot afternoons, I listened to the muted echo of the wooden camel bells on the necks of doe-eyed camels that passed my house. Nomad women would often stop and ask for water. They had heard that the Saad Musa had adopted me, a white woman, and therefore tribal relations had the right to ask me for water. The camels would stand patiently in a line, loaded with the *aqual* (the portable round Somali house) and the bags of supplies the women had come to the village to buy. If by some chance my gasoline refrigerator had been running long enough to make ice, I would put an ice cube in the glass of water I brought out to the women, just to see the reaction.

"What is this?" the willowy women would ask, eyeing the clear object floating on the top of the water with suspicion.

"It's ice," I would tell them in a well-practiced Somali phrase. Most people had heard of ice and would eagerly reach into the glass to take it into their hands.

"No, this is hot!" they would shout. "It's burning me!" they would cry, frightened by the unexpected touch of the modern world and dropping the opaque cube.

"*Wallahi*, it's just a little water," I would explain, oh so innocently, as it melted into a little circle on the hot earth. The ice disappeared into the dry desert soil without a trace, but I fear other effects of the modern world on this little county will not disappear so easily.

The Somali nomads have a saying: "The last camel in line walks as quickly as the first." We live on one small planet. What happens to the least of us will have an effect on the rest of us. I hope that the stories in this book will impress upon you something of the grace and beauty of the people who once lived in the small village of Arabsiyo in Northern Somalia.

Donni Maayo

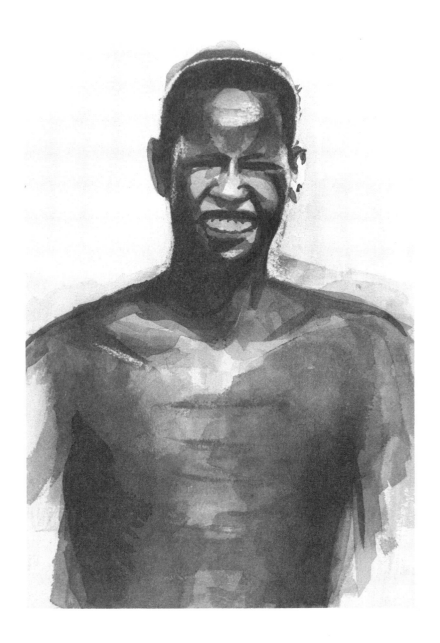

*I bade you farewell. Wished
you a journey full of blessing.
Every hour that you exist,
when you go to sleep
and when you awake,
Keep in mind the troth
between us.
I am waiting for you,
come safely back,
come safely back.*

—Mohammed Tukaale

"There it is!" said Ali.
Disappointment and fear clamped my
windpipe shut and squeezed the breath
right out of me. I fought to conceal my
reaction and to keep my mouth from
flapping open in utter despair. Ali Esa,
the Somali driver, was taking me in a
Land Rover to the village of Arabsiyo,
my first teaching post. He pointed to a
scraggly group of round, beehive-shaped
nomadic houses built of woven mats and
arched poles. They sat silently amid the
blowing dust and thorny acacia trees of
the desert. The huts, called *aquals* in
Somali, were grey and weather-beaten.

They were surrounded by a low fence built of branches. Silent children, wearing only ragged shirts and leather amulets, watched us with flies crawling in their eyes. There were so many flies that they didn't even bother to swat them away. I glanced at Ali who was laughing at me. "No, that's just some nomads," he chortled, enjoying my obvious sigh of relief. Ali could not understand why anyone (especially a woman) would come from the United States to live in a small village in Somalia. My father had the same opinion, half a world away. He had been horrified that I chose to join the Peace Cops rather than take a job and earn good money after I finished college. "Some people like elephant meat," he said from behind his newspaper. "Myself, I can't stomach it."

Early that morning, Ali and I had passed the twin hills called *Nasa Habloid*, the Woman's Breasts, on the outskirts of Hargeisa, and headed northwest to Arabsiyo, in the direction of the Ethiopian border. Hargeisa is the capital city of the Northern region of Somalia. In most Third World countries it would be considered a backwater outpost; in Somalia it was a major city.

I couldn't truthfully say that Ali and I had been bouncing along the rough road that runs from Hargeisa to Arabsiyo. Bounce implies somewhat of a soft landing. No, we had been hurtling (emphasis on the first four letters) along the rugged path for over three hours. Several times we had gone down the steep sides of dry river beds where the road stopped in its tracks. Ali raced through the sand at the bottom of the gully to keep the Land Rover from becoming mired in the loose sand, and obstinately bumped back up the other side of the *tuug*.

The Somali desert is lunar looking, its dry coarse soil punctuated here and there with shrubs and thorn bushes. Somalia was called affectionately "the armpit of the world" by the expatriate community. Most foreigners lived in insulated compounds and socialized very little with native Somalis. However, they prided themselves in the cheerful endurance of hardship, a trait they had copied from the local population. It was either that or constant grumbling,

4

and there were those who succumbed to that. The Puntite Kings of ancient Egypt named the Northern region of Somalia "The Land of Punt," God's Land. However in 1968, when Sargent Shriver visited with the first Peace Corps Washington staff, it was referred to as "The Land God Forgot." How does one explain this difference in opinion between the Puntite Kings and Peace Corps Washington? Does God challenge us to grow spiritually? Then Somalia is God's land of challenge. If God rewards the faithful with material wealth, then Somalia is the land that God forgot.

Early Arab traders referred to it as the "Land of Milk and Myrrh" based on the Somali custom of welcoming strangers with a beverage of milk, and burning myrrh to release its sweet odor. The Somali word for the act of milking is *soo mal*, milk is a basic food of the nomadic herdsmen, hence the modern name of the country, Somalia. There were perhaps six million Somali people and their major occupation was animal herding. Despite the sparse population density, any time Ali stopped the Land Rover so I could pee, some nomad would appear out of nowhere and interrupt my moment of relief. He would stand silently leaning on his stick while I jumped up midstream and struggled to pull up my soggy pants.

The tire ruts Ali followed led over one last hill, and there, sunning itself in the afternoon's brilliant azure sky, was Arabsiyo. It was a charming little village! The houses were white with corrugated metal roofs and indigo blue designs on the walls. There was a main street with a splendid mosque complete with a minaret and gleaming white tiles, several small shops, and a marketplace. There were about fifty houses neatly arranged around the center of town. The hills beyond the village were decorated with gardens which appeared lush and green from the distance, in sharp contrast to the endless sienna of the desert. The gardens were irrigated by hand from deep wells. On the other side of the *tuug* stood two school buildings and a small dispensary. The intermediate school had just been completed with U.S. Aid materials and local labor. I would work in the new school with two Somali teachers.

It was exactly what I had fantasized about before leaving my home and frantic father in the Midwest. A little village in Africa: no electricity and no running water. Water was a precious commodity which the Somalis used with great care and grave attention. I quickly became obsessed with it and hoarded my dirty water in case of emergency (whenever I had a container). There was no telephone or telegraph. Once each week a trade truck might come from Hargeisa, bringing supplies, news if there was any, maybe a letter, perhaps a friend. There were no other vehicles in the town, only a few scattered donkeys. There were plenty of goats, sheep, cattle, and camels, the basic unit of the social and economic system of Somali life. I was the first foreigner to live in Arabsiyo. I did not know that I would also be the last.

I had heard John Kennedy describe his concept of the Peace Corps in the fall of 1960, on the steps of the University of Michigan Union in Ann Arbor. He said that young Americans were ready to accept the challenge of world peace and were willing to serve in the farthest parts of the globe to promote love and understanding among nations. I was fourteen years old and had come to see the presidential candidate during a weekend visit with my sister, Susan, a math student at U. of M. We heard that Kennedy would be spending the night on campus and had waited to see him. Discouraged when he was hours late, we left to go home.

My sister's apartment was not far away from the Michigan Union on State Street, and late that night, for a lark, we went back. At fourteen, I was thrilled to be out after ten o'clock at night. There were no stars in the still, cold darkness of the long Michigan night. Big clouds of our glistening white breath reflected in the street lights. The crowd had thinned considerably by the time we returned, and we moved through the people up to the frozen steps of the student union. The air was heavy with dampness and it crept into your bones and wouldn't let go for hours. Suddenly the lights of the Kennedy cavalcade beamed in the distance. When they stopped in front of the building, the silver smoke of the cars' exhaust billowed out into the street like panting black stallions. Kennedy jumped out, and hurried up the grey stone steps surrounded by nervous secret servicemen. He paused as he was about to enter the building, turned and waved at the crowd. He said goodnight, then, perhaps because of the late hour and the loyal crowd who had waited so long in the chill, he decided to say a few words. He joked that we must be crazy, standing there in that frigid night. Then it seemed that he looked at me for a moment, and he began to talk about service in the cause of world peace. At least that is how I remember it, he looked at me. At fourteen all things are possible, even John Kennedy asking a little girl to try living in a foreign country and bring peace into the world.

My mother had died in a car accident and I needed a cause, a reason, something to fill up the empty places inside of me. After she died I was suddenly not a child any longer. Motherless children can no longer remain children. You need to have a loving mother in order to trust and love like a child. Motherless children wonder about suffering and why God doesn't hear your prayers anymore, or if he ever did. After her death, I was no longer interested in sleep-over parties and poodle skirts. Life seemed pointless until John Kennedy gave me a challenge I could dream about. He offered me an escape from a place where mothers die and fathers drink to numb the pain. I was young and thought that bringing peace into some desperate corner of the world will bring it into my desperate heart as well. My sister went on to NASA and she worked on the moon shot. I signed up for the Peace Corps in 1968 and went to a place where time stood still, rooted in the rhythmic waltz of camels across the blowing sand.

Peace and understanding were a large part of the vision intended by Sargent Shiver and the very first Peace Corps staff. However, Peace Corps service really had little to do with the policy makers in Washington. Policies don't have much effect in places without plumbing. When I went over the last little knoll into Arabsiyo, it did not matter anymore what the people in Washington, or even those in the Peace

Corps office in Hargeisa, said or did. The only thing that mattered was that I was there and the Somalis were there. We would grow in understanding and misunderstanding every day, but we would grow with each other. There was only one truck a week, and even that came only during the dry season.

I was prepared for my conquest of Arabsiyo with a battered suitcase and a smattering of the Somali language. Language instruction is one of the most important parts of Peace Corps training programs. The method used during my training was total immersion. This technique is helpful in getting Americans who have never spoken a foreign language before to feel comfortable sounding like cretins. The Peace Corps took over an old hotel in upstate New York and told all the eager new recruits that they could only speak Somali. The only words anyone knew were Somalia, Mogadishu, the capital of the country, and Hargeisa. We eagerly latched on to any vocabulary we learned in class and used it under a variety of circumstances. If I knew the word for tea, then it would have to do when I wanted soda or coffee.

We were greeted early in the morning with bells and rolled out of bed muttering "Mogadishu" under our breath. I have never been one to talk much during breakfast, so it didn't bother me that I had to grunt for the coffee, cream, and sugar. Language classes were taught by native speakers who used oral pattern drills. Nothing was translated into English. The meaning of the phrases was conveyed by highly innovative methods. For example, our Somali instructor held up a picture of the famous balcony scene in Romeo and Juliet. Pointing to Romeo, who was standing in the street looking up at the window for Juliet, he repeated: *"Juliet, Juliet, hygate chog-ta?"* Then Juliet appeared on the balcony and answered Romeo in Somali: *"Romeo, Romeo, hulcan ban chog-ga."* No explanation was offered and I simply assumed that Somali people called out, "where for art thou?" if they were looking for someone. Skits and pictures were used, nothing was translated. We were encouraged to learn Somali in the same way that a baby acquires language, directly. We were forced to think in Somali. The problem with this method of language acquisition is that while you may sound wonderful, you often don't know what you are saying. On my second day in Arabsiyo I learned the hard way about the hazards of thinking you were thinking in Somali. When what I said wasn't what I thought I said, I had no way to stop getting what I had asked for, but didn't want.

Ali took me to the little house he had arranged for me to rent. It was similar to the other thirty houses in the village. It had two rooms, a tin roof, and packed dirt floors. It looked like a palace after the huts in the desert. The villagers were farmers and lived in square houses rather than the portable huts used by the nomads outside of the towns. My headmaster, Abdillahi, appeared attracted by the crowd of small boys running after the Land Rover. He shouted at the women who had appeared in doorways to see what all the commotion was about to sweep out "my" house for me. After the dust had settled, we all went to the tea shop for tea. We sat under a big tree at rickety tables outside the shed containing the kitchen. I dreaded the moment when Ali would announce that he had to go, but dread doesn't slow down time. He dropped me back at the house in the late afternoon. I went inside and shut the door but stood right there and listened to the sound of the Land Rover until it was devoured by the desert, irretrievably gone. I felt so alone that I decided my father had been right about this Peace Corps business after all. I wished that I could tell him and my throat welled shut thinking about it. That quiet moment of solitude didn't last long, and in later days I remembered it rather fondly. It was as if the village were a female lion, sitting on its haunches and waiting for the male to finish eating its fill. As soon as that dust cloud from the Peace Corps Land Rover dissipated back into the desert, I belonged to Arabsiyo.

As darkness fell, quickly and with resounding finality, I longed for electricity like a woman longs for her lover. I had only a small lantern that I lit with trembling fingers. Then I sat right in the faint circle of light afraid to move. Far away, I heard what sounded like controlled screaming. It grew closer and closer and I realized that a crowd of the villagers was coming in my direction. I wondered if I were going to be killed by the excited crowd pounding on my flimsy door. I wrote, "this is it" in my diary, then "what is this?" then I crossed everything out, feeling rather foolish about my shaking hands and pounding heart. I heard, *"Calli, calli, wa arrose!"* but I could not think what the words meant. I opened the door with trembling limbs and was pulled into the street by a throng of laughing women. Suddenly a tall and slender woman was at my side, holding on to my arm and guiding me into the street. "Come, come with us, it's a wedding!" she said into my ear with a decidedly British accent. I grabbed onto this new friend as if she were my long lost sister. She spoke English! I was so excited and relieved that I would be able to talk to someone in the village .

"My name is Asha and I learned to speak English in London," she told me gaily as we moved along in the circle of women. "My friend Assia is getting married," Asha continued but I could barely hear her because of the excited screaming and dancing of the crowd of women who swirled around us. Asha seemed calm and serene despite the commotion, she moved with grace and presence as if she were a queen.

"Where do you live?" I asked, already desperate to visit Asha as soon as possible.

"In Hargeisa," she responded with a warm smile. "I will come and visit with you soon," she reassured me, smiling at my terrified eyes.

"Hargeisa!" I whined, "but it's so far from here and I really want to talk to you."

Asha squeezed both of my hands warmly, "Sorry but I need to go to the bride right now, I will see you soon!" she said reassuringly. "Have fun tonight!" she said with a little wave, then she disappeared into the darkness.

I was quickly drawn into the crowd dancing in front of a fire and I felt bereft for the second time that day. It is amazing how lonely one can feel right in the middle of a group of people who want to entertain you. The entire village seemed pleased that I had come to the celebration, the first of many events I would attend as the admittedly strange but nevertheless honored guest. Watching the excited dancing and singing around the fire, I could feel the pulse of a people free from the veneer of Western civilization. They danced as if they were heavy into the drug of being without pretense. It frightened my intellectual way of coping with the world, and I shrank back from the celebration and returned to my little house. I endured a restless sleep in the narrow bed that I had pulled 12 inches away from the wall to discourage cockroaches, scorpions, and snakes from crawling up and dropping in.

I awoke that first morning to find my bed surrounded. I heard a noise, and when I opened my eyes to see what it was, I jumped and sat up in bed with a start. Five women and a strange looking young man stared at me, then everyone but the odd youth laughed at my surprise. He stood staring out of vacant eyes and shifting from side to side. It was readily apparent that he was not mentally alert. Obviously privacy had a different meaning in this little village. The tallest of the women stood a little apart as if she were not really one of the group. She had wide set eyes and a bold manner, she laughed openly like a man not with a girlish giggle. She pointed to herself and said, "Chamis." She pointed meaningfully at me.

I quickly grasped that she wanted to know my name. "Jeanne," I said pointing at myself. Then, "Chamis," pointing at her. This caused an explosion of laughter and the women swished sinuously out of the room chattering like a flock of birds. Somali women almost never hurry, they sway like wheat fields in the wind.

"Hassan N'Asse, calli," Chamis said calling to the strange young man who obediently followed her out of the room. He seemed to have forgotten all about me and why he had come, if he ever did understand. He mumbled and bit his lips as he ambled out behind Chamis' swaying backside.

I realized they had been curious and had come for a look at the stranger while she was sleeping, and it was safe. Only the woman called Chamis had been bold enough to

11

speak to me and I wondered why she seemed different from the others, and if she took care of Hassan N'Asse. I wondered if I would be able to ask Asha about them or if she had already returned to Hargeisa. I had not met anyone else who spoke enough English to have a conversation with and my Somali was practically non-existent.

Soon, the word was out that I was awake and hot tea arrived from the tea shop, along with some cold, flat, pancakes, made of millet and called *lahough*. I didn't know who ordered it, it just arrived. Ahmed, the tea shop boy, shyly entered the room and placed them on my little table without daring to look at me. He had such long arms and legs that he looked like a puppet, all joints, no muscle. He was nervous and jumped when the tin plate banged against the table. He fished the only fork in town out from behind his ear, and ran out the door.

The pancakes had a tangy taste but I could not eat them because they were covered with an enormous glob of cold camel-butter, *ghee*. It had the most rancid taste and smell that had ever entered my nasal passages. The smell was so strong it made me wince. I nibbled around the edges of the pancakes on parts that were not coated with *ghee* and left the rest on the battered tin plate. No matter how hungry I was, I never could eat anything coated with *ghee*. The tea, however, was wonderful. It was hot and flavored with cardamom, and was laced with plenty of sugar and milk. The milk had a charcoal taste and it added a slightly smokey flavor to the tea. The Somali use burning coals to sterilize the inside of milk containers because water is scarce. It tasted odd at first but I grew to like it well enough.

The strong unguarded morning sunlight encouraged me to examine my surroundings. No detail escapes the mighty sun in Somalia, everything is revealed without the compassion of shadows. My house was painted a light blue and had been decorated with white diamond shapes which waltzed around the outside walls at eye level. The roof, covering the two rooms and the entrance, was rippled tin. A diminutive walled courtyard went around the back of both rooms. An out-house, placed at one side of the courtyard, was called a "longdrop" because it was so deep: the 12-foot depth kept odors down at the bottom. A cooking shed was located on the other side of the courtyard. The floors were packed earth. I could see that the kitchen was a low-maintenance model. I would never have to scrub the kitchen floor. There were no counter tops to wipe, no refrigerator to empty, no drawers to stick, and no sink to clog. I was not going to have to worry about soap scum in the shower since there wasn't one. Just think, I mused, looking into the deep hole that served as my toilet, no flushing, no toilet paper. The Somalis keep a bowl of water in the long drop and reserve the left hand for personal hygiene. I am left-handed and they were always shocked when I ate with my unclean hand. Each room had two small windows on opposite sides, with blue wooden shutters to close for privacy. There was no glass or screens so I wouldn't have to worry about finding someone who "did windows." Nothing fit quite right, you could see the sky through sections of the roof, and the shutters didn't meet, but it would have to do. I felt as though I had moved into our old garage.

My housekeeping chores completed, I decided to stroll though the village to get to know it a little better, and emerged as casually as I could manage from my little house. The streets were wide dusty tracks and the houses were all similar to mine on the outside. They consisted of two small square rooms built side by side, with an entranceway in the middle and a courtyard in the back. The walls were made of sun-baked bricks and smoothed by a layer of whitewash. There were five rows of houses and a main street of five diminutive general stores and several tea shops. A small outdoor marketplace was located just at the edge of the shops. A picturesque mosque guarded the entrance to the town and the souls of the inhabitants. I knew women were not allowed into the mosque but drew close that first day in order to admire it. I wanted to see the open architecture and the beautiful mosaic floor within. However, merely crossing the street caused quite a stir. Anger appeared on the faces of men and there was fear in the eyes of the women who watched. I decided not to begin my residency by arousing such a commotion and walked away as quickly as I could. I never approached the mosque again during the time I lived in Arabsiyo.

I began to realize that I was not going to be able to maintain a low profile. My morning stroll through town had taken about five minutes, given the size of the town, but I had managed to attract about twenty children, several laughing women, and some older boys. This group was quite interested in my every movement and commented about everything I did or even looked at. Every now and then children would run up and touch me, then run off laughing, proud of the courage they demonstrated by touching the "Bis Corpus," as they pronounced it. For the first time in my life I realized what life is like for the ultra famous. Comments and interpretations are made about everything you do. This is not fun when you are trying to explore, not entertain. I would have liked to sit in the tea shop for more of the delicious tea, but was embarrassed about the large and rowdy crowd following me. A quiet cup of tea would not be possible. Women did not drink tea in public, and I was worried that approaching the tea shop would result in the same sort of reaction that had occurred when I had gone to look at the mosque. I was beginning to feel a little helpless. I wanted some tea but couldn't think how to get it.

I headed back to my house in resignation and noticed a group of older boys at the edge of town. They had slingshots made out of goat hide and were whirling them over their heads and throwing rocks. I stopped, with the crowd at my heels, to watch. I thought they might be some of my students because they were dressed in the school uniform of khaki shorts and white shirts. I didn't know how to ask, "Are you students at the school?" so I watched and hoped they knew a little English. They stopped the game so I greeted them in Somali with, *"Ma nabut bah."* This utterance was followed by gasps and then a ripple of excitement went through the crowd. Since I could say hello, everyone assumed that I spoke Somali fluently. Many of the women began to ululate, which is the high pitched vibrating scream that had frightened me so much the previous evening. I cannot make this sound and have never met a Western person who could. The tongue flutters against the roof of the mouth and Midwestern appendages won't flap like that.

One boy stepped forward and boldly said "Good morning, I am Ali Abdi," in halting English as if he had never spoken out loud in English before. He was about fourteen and was a little rounder than the other boys. His shirt was clean and he wore leather sandals, unlike most people, who were barefoot. I assumed that his family must have some money. Ali Abdi's face was dominated by the biggest, softest, brown eyes I had ever seen and I was immediately entranced. He did not venture any other phrases and I knew without a doubt that we had both exhausted the words we knew in each other's language.

The other boys were beaming with pride about my interest in their slingshots, and demonstrated that they were shooting at birds flying overhead. I love birds and have been a bird watcher for several years. I was not pleased to see them being used for target practice. After I realized what the boys were shooting at, I decided not to watch any further. I was afraid that any attention would escalate their efforts to bag a bird on the wing. However I did pause so Ali Abdi could show me a little brown bird he had caught. He proudly warbled on about it in unintelligible Somali and I searched my limited vocabulary for a response. At that point I said something I would regret later: I admired his catch. *"Won axion,"* I said smiling at him. "Good, good, that's a nice bird." In the Western world we have a habit of admiring things that belong to other people; it is a compliment to the owner. What a beautiful dress, dog, or house, we murmur. In Somalia if you admire something it is considered a request that must be honored. The dress will be delivered, the dog handed over, the comment about the house met with shock. The limp bird was thrust into my hands and I refused it to the dismay of earnest Ali Abdi. His big brown eyes filled with confusion as he stood there holding out the bird. I decided I had better return to my house and think things over a bit and quickly strolled away.

Having spent the better part of 30 minutes in a quiet (?) stroll through town, I waved goodby to the crowd that had gathered outside my door and bid them firmly, *"Nabut gilio."* This aroused more commentary and I could see that returning to my house and telling them goodby was not going to disperse the fringe elements in Somali society. They were settling down in the street, discussing the events of the last half-hour and were obviously intrigued. They were waiting to see what would happen next. I undid the bolt from my door and entered the cool darkness. I leaned against the rough bricks and realized with a sinking feeling that this was not going to be easy. It was 8:30 in the morning and I was trapped.

I had no choice but to sit inside the house with the doors and windows closed for a while and wait for things to settle down. I felt confident, however, that the crowd would soon tire of sitting outside and would head off to waiting jobs and responsibilities.

The silence was broken by a sharp knock on the thin wooden door followed by loud wailing. Alarmed, I quickly unbolted my door and found a woman firmly holding a struggling little boy in front of her. She shoved him at me, shouting, *"Shedun! Shedun!* (Devil! Devil!)" His dark chestnut eyes grew large with fear and amazement as he registered my white skin and red hair. He screamed in total terror and struggled to hide himself in the folds of his mother's long dress, and billowing slip. I knelt down to reassure him that I was not really the devil, but she snatched him away from my outstretched hand. Then, she triumphantly stalked proudly off with her screaming baby. I heard the satisfied laughter from the crowd still lingering outside my door. This little boy had been told that if he didn't mind he would be taken to the devil. I could just imagine what was being shouted at little boys who threw goat dung at their sisters: " Stop that, Mohammed, or I'll take you over to the devil's house right this minute." This maniacal mother had done just that. In Africa the devil is white, and there I was, white and scary, conveniently located in the house down the street, ready to terrorize naughty little children. I slammed my door shut in disgust. Years later I read a letter to Ann Landers from a policeman who complained about the same thing, parents who used him to threaten their children. "Stop that or the _____ will take you away," must be a part of the collective unconscious of parents throughout the world.

Being a celebrity was one thing, being used as a threat and punishment for little children was another. I felt more than a little used and angry. I had not fretted long when there was another knock at the door. I banged it open and shouted, "That's enough!" expecting another mother who dared to torment her baby. Ahmed, the scrawny boy from the tea shop, had come to collect the breakfast dishes. He shrank back from my blazing eyes and flaming face. His long arms were up and ready to protect himself from the devil's rage. The crowd of little boys and women hovering just outside the door were highly amused by Ahmed's fear of the shouting *Bis Corpus*. They beamed with satisfaction at having been clever enough to have found the best show in town.

I motioned for Ahmed to enter and glared at the crowd, much to their amusement. Ahmed would not be consoled by my attempts at Somali. He darted into the house, scooped up the plates and tea thermos and dashed away with the clattering tin dishes. He dropped the precious fork but wouldn't even stop to pick it up. There would be no late morning tea for me from the tea shop.

I threw myself on my bed feeling totally lost, and my frustrated anger soon dissolved into hot tears. I struggled to control my sobs so they would not be heard outside. When my eyes adjusted to the darkness, I blinked back scalding tears to look at the shuttered window above my bed. The cracks of the roughly made shutters revealed several pairs of alert mahogany eyes. I could hear the little boys at the window describing the scene within to those too dignified to climb up on the ledge and peer in the cracks. I threw my shoe at the window. I had had enough of being a goodwill ambassador for America. So much for world peace, this called for violence.

I went into the other room where the shutters met each other a little better thinking I would at least deprive the little bastards of an easy look. I paced the floor. What does one do in an empty little room with a dirt floor, no shower, no telephone, no television, radio, record player, food, books, newspapers, nail polish, or mirror, no tea, and no exit? Just before I left Hargeisa, Bill, the Peace Corps doctor, had passed out little boxes of dental floss to the volunteers. He demonstrated how to use it and recommended it as a way to pass the time in one's post. I considered flossing my teeth, but decided I had better save it so I would have something to look forward to.

Amina, my next-door neighbor, grew tired of the jostling horde outside. I listened with relief as she shooed everyone away. She chased the little boys with threats and the women with sarcasm and a few stones. She stood staunchly outside my door with her hands on her hips until the women left. The little boys retreated around the corners of the houses hoping she would leave. I opened the door and she entered, the faint smell of musky incense pleasing my nose as her long dress or *dira* swayed around her. She had a perfectly oval face, ginger skin, and intelligent cheerful eyes. She was one of those resourceful people who can size up a situation instantly and respond without effort. She lectured me for a moment with a hennaed finger pointed at the door, but soon realized I could not understand what she was saying.

"*Cha?*" she asked, sympathetically. Would I like some tea?

"Yes," I nodded, feeling like a child needing its mother. I needed someone to teach me, to protect me, to feed me. I was beginning to realize that I was helpless. I did not know how to get water or food or how to light my lamps at night. I couldn't order tea or even chase pesky little boys away. I was fearful of growing dependant on Amina but I had no alternative. After all, what did she get out of this?

"*Wallahi wa ruiaad!*" "Really, this is quite a show!" she laughed as she shimmered out to the empty street. I realized what Amina was getting out of her new neighbor.

She returned with the tea, and Ali Abdi (the boy who had tried to give me the little brown bird) came in behind her with a burlap sack. He seemed to know Amina and she explained in very simple Somali that he was her husband's younger brother. His father and her father-in-law was Ali Yare. Ali Yare owned a shop in town. Ali Abdi watched carefully while Amina pointed to herself, then to him, then in the direction of town. When I nodded that I understood the relationship he reached inside the bag and shyly offered me another gift. It was a male sunbird killed by Ali's slingshot. The beak was long and slender, it bent downward and was similar to an American hummingbird. The limp bird was iridescent green with a little bronze shading and bright yellow feathers on the sides. I was touched at his attempt to present me with the gift of another bird, yet I was quite dismayed. I certainly was not going to eat the sunbird, if that is what he meant. Stunned, I tried to think of something to say.

I had learned the phrase, *"Donni maayo kan ookale"* in a skit about someone who is saying: "No, don't give me any more." I clearly repeated the phrase, he nodded in apparent understanding, and ran off leaving the pathetic pile of feathers outside my door. I was quite pleased with myself for communicating so clearly and felt that things had taken a turn for the better. I sat down to savor a glass of tea and my success.

My confidence was a bit shaken a little while later when Ali Abdi returned with a friend and yet another dead bird. They offered a weaver bird, with yellowish plumage, a greenish back, and wings with black bars. It was another male, with a black mask. It was offered quite proudly to me, a limp heap of bedraggled feathers. It looked as though it had only been wounded by the slingshot and then stamped to death as it struggled to flee. I was trapped again. I did not want to insult the boys, but I decidedly did not want to encourage my students to kill these beautiful birds as gifts for me. I did not want to encourage any more slingshots aimed at pleasing the teacher. I sorted through the Somali phrases we had learned. *"Romeo, Romeo hygate chog ta?"*

would not help. The only phrase I knew was: *"Donni maayo kan ookale."* This time I repeated, *"Donni maayo kan ookale!"* several times, making sure they knew what I said. They ran off, holding hands and laughing. The laughter worried me, but I had no idea what else I could say to the boys.

I couldn't believe it only minutes later when I answered the door: two angular boys in khaki shorts, dirty white shirts and bare feet were standing there, offering me a hoopoe. I was horrified. I love birds (*live* birds) this was the first hoopoe I had ever seen, and it had been killed for nothing. It was unmistakable with tawny brown plumage interspersed with pink, a long curved beak, a crest, white wings and a tail with black stripes. This time I yelled, my voice full of indignation and anger, *"Donni maayo kan ookale!, kan ookale, kan ookale!"* I ended by slamming the door for the second time that day while I shouted *"maaya,"* no. I paced around my tiny room, trying to recall any other possible phrase. I frantically looked through my notes, but wildlife massacre had not been a topic in my language training classes.

The boys were gone quite a while and I was hopeful that they had finally stopped the dreadful game. However, when I heard the knock, opened the door, and saw the gorgeous eurasian bee-eater, I knew that whatever I said was making things worse, not better. This elegant bird was brown and yellow on the back, the wings and tail were blue green. The beak was ebony, long and thin, but it had been smashed in a death stomp. I was overcome with helplessness, a bee-eater, dead for nothing. I shook my head sadly and refused this latest offering with anguish. "O please *donni maayo kan ookale,"* I said. Sadly I refused the poor thing with a wave, and the boys left it sprawled in the dust outside my door. It lay along with the other dead birds, all executed with a slingshot in this game of international misunderstanding. I was somehow causing an ecological disaster, nothing I said stopped the slaughter. I was having a terrific impact on the animals living around this poor little village, they were being slaughtered to please the teacher. I considered going out and confiscating the silly slingshots, but was fearful of what that would look like to the crowd that lurked in the shadows, ready for some more excitement. Where was Greenpeace when I needed them? "Greenpeace, Greenpeace, *hygate chog ta?*" I muttered to the long drop.

The next knock on my door was Abdillahi, my headmaster. He had brought two other teachers from the school to meet me. They had been in Hargeisa when I arrived, and had just returned on the trade truck. Abdillahi was an officious man. A little shorter than most of the very tall and elegant Somalis, he made up in bossiness what he lacked in height. Abdul Kader, the other teacher at the secondary school, was cautious about speaking English. His personality became much more aggressive in Somali, and he often argued with Abdillahi. In English he was quiet and reserved. He watched carefully, eyeing me respectfully. His shirt and *ma'aweiss* were so neat he looked rather preppy except for the frayed edges of his shirt collar. Subti was a jewel. He had studied English at ENTEC, a Somali college in the South, and spoke it fluently and easily. He was not too tall and had a tribal scar on the left side of his face. It was a long line from the temple to the jaw with small marks on either side. He had a generous mouth which filled his face when he smiled, which was often. His eyes were dancing with amusement at Abdillahi's ridiculous English and his officious manner.

"Where your father?" said Abdillahi gruffly. "I must talk him. I am taking care of you in this village. You are lowly here without your people."

Subti watched me blanche slightly at Abdillahi's remarks, and smiled at me knowingly. Here at last was a friend. Someone who could see Abdillahi's absurdity from my perspective. Abdul Kader had no idea what was happening, and stood shuffling from one foot to another. He had on new brown leather sandals, the mark of a teacher. Poor people wore the rubber beach thongs, or *daas*, until the soles were as thin as paper.

Abdillahi began to rummage through the meager possessions I had spread out on my rickety metal table. He picked up my flashlight and announced he would need this as the headmaster of the school. Alarmed at being more in the dark than I already was, I protested. He looked at me scornfully but announced he would return it that evening. I could see there was no point in pushing the issue any further, and I didn't know what good a flashlight was going to do me anyway. Suddenly there was another knock at my door. Abdillahi looked at me accusingly as if I should not be having visitors that he did not know about. He turned to answer the door and I followed him, to my door, to see who had come to see me.

It was Ali Abdi and the other boys again, and this time they had killed a barbet, I could see its large bill and bright red feathers. Abdillahi shouted at them, cursing half in English and the rest in Somali. They ran off, leaving the poor barbet in the dust with the pile of other birds outside my house. "Why are those stupid boys bring you dead birds?" he rumbled at me. "I see boys all over town killing anything that flies! Why you want all these birds for?"

"The boys are making me gifts, except I told them that I don't want the birds," I explained hopelessly. "They have been coming all day with different birds and I can't make them understand that I don't want any birds," I said, more to Subti than Abdillahi. I hoped he could unravel the mystery of the little gifts that wouldn't end.

"They are ignorant boys from the bush," retorted Abdillahi. "Just tell them to go away and leave you alone."

I was afraid that Abdillahi would punish the boys when they had tried so hard to please me all afternoon. However I felt incapable of explaining why they had continued bringing the different birds.

"What did you say to the boys?" asked Subti, facing me with interest. "Every boy in town has been out all day with slingshots shooting at anything that moves."

"I said, *Donni maayo kan ookale.*" There was a long silence and I wondered what I was mispronouncing. I looked first at Subti, then at Abdillahi, finally at Abdul Kader. They looked back at me strangely. "I said that each time they came back with another bird."

Subti and Abdillahi both began to laugh suddenly, and

ended up dancing around the barren little room slapping each other in hilarity. Subti explained something to Abdul Kader in Somali and he too joined the little laughing party, pointing at me and the birds laying in a row outside my door. "You told the boys, 'Don't bring me another one *like that*,'" said Subti finally. "No wonder they brought you all those different birds! They were trying to find out which bird would please the new *Bis Corpus* teacher. These boys have been running all over the place trying to shoot down the exact bird the American teacher wants to eat!"

Abdillahi screwed up his face and peered into mine as if he were trying to see what was the matter with me. "Where you learn to speak Somali?" he asked.

"Well, our classes were in New York," I began to explain, but he had heard enough. He rolled his eyes as if that explained the problem. To Abdillahi, people in New York just didn't speak Somali very well, and I couldn't dispute that. They scooted out the door, still laughing. I wondered how I was ever going to make sense out of what was going on around me. I had a large impact on the village and I didn't have any way of understanding it, much less controlling it. I hoped that Asha would come back and visit with me very soon. I realized that I would either have to learn enough of the language to figure things out or meet Somalis who spoke English. I had to admit though that even speaking English did not seem to explain much. I decided to console myself by flossing my teeth. It was a consolation I was to repeat many times in "The Land of Punt."

Shifta

It is only with the heart that one can see rightly. What is essential is invisible to the eye.

— Antoine De Saint-Exupery

The African clock is internal. It keeps time with the daylight and the starlight, the hunger of the people, and what needs to be done. It is not an external clock, that hangs on the wall and compels us to eat even if we are not hungry, or to leave because it is time and not because we want to go. Sometimes time passes slowly, sometimes so much happens in an instant that it takes years to understand it. I had such an instant on a truck one sultry afternoon. I wanted to get from Hargeisa back to my post in the little town of Arabsiyo. I had been in Hargeisa for a few days to arrange for teaching supplies to be shipped to my school.

I also spent sereral pleasant afternoons with Asha, a young woman I first met at a wedding in Arabsiyo, but I needed to get back to my school so classes could begin.

This intersection of the Western conception of time as absolute, inflexible, and outside of us, and the African sense of time as meaningful, flexible, and related to the situation at hand, can pose serious problems for the traveller in Somalia. It is especially troublesome when one wants to know what time the transport truck or car will leave for the desired destination. *"Enshallah"* or When God wills, is the cheerful answer. It does not make the least amount of sense to the driver that (given the uncertainty you perceive in his answer) you choose to stand next to the lorry as it is being loaded and wait. He does not understand that you are fearful it might leave without you and that it is the only way you have to get where you need to go. To the Somali, the truck will not leave until it has been loaded, and that is the time when it will leave. If you are part of the load, it is obvious that it will not leave until you are on the truck. Instead of fretting about nothing, I was told to go have some tea in town. The answer to my question, "What time should I come back?" was equally obvious to any Somali.

"When you are finished with the tea, of course."

In Somalia one begins to live in the present. The sun always sets at precisely six thirty because it is so close to the equator. The sun rises at the same hour each day and casts its shadow in the same places in the room at the same time each day. It reached the left end of the table that stood by my bed at seven each morning. If I got up when the sun reached the third tile from the wall in my bedroom, and left when it reached my door, I would be on time for school which always began after the teachers had finished drinking their morning tea.

Freed from watching hands endlessly chasing each other around a numbered dial, I began to consider time in terms of the unfolding drama of life: I knew that the trade truck would leave only after it had been loaded. If it were the rainy season, the driver would want to reach his destination before the late afternoon when the rains come.

Therefore, he would leave the market place in Hargeisa before the midmorning prayers.

Salat, the prayer of the faithful, is one of the five pillars of Islam. It takes the place of a wristwatch in the life of Somali believers. It offers the real timetable for the day, and reminds the faithful that humankind is intended for more than working and eating. In Hargeisa, as in all major towns in Somalia, the call to prayers is given by the *muezzin.* His call drifts over the crowded camel market like the distant pealing of church bells. He tells the faithful, and the unfaithful alike, that God is great, Mohammed is his prophet, and the time for *salat* has come. All the business of the town ceases at the call to worship, so the driver will want to have the truck loaded by that time.

> "O ye who believe! When the call is heard for the prayer of the day...haste unto remembrance of Allah and leave your trading." (Sura 62:9)

There are forty-seven boxes, fifteen sacks of grain, seven baskets of oranges, and four chickens that have to be loaded on the truck. If I go to the tea shop and have one cup of spiced sweet tea, the truck will be loaded and ready to leave when I get back. Allah only knows what time that will be, but that is God's problem and not mine. I understand when the truck will leave, and it has nothing to do with numbers, and everything to do with life.

Trade trucks in Somalia are the central means of transportation. Boxes of rice and flour, cloth, tins of kerosene, bags of grain, boxes of fruits and vegetables are piled into the back of the truck. Human cargo rides on top of the supplies. The riders stand or sit depending on the size of the load. For a few extra shillings I could ride in the cab with the driver, but there is only one such seat. Usually I was exposed to the burning sun and endless dust curling its insistent way into every crevice of my body as I sat on the back of the truck. Trucks are not plentiful in Somalia. Working trucks that run with four tires are even more rare. Most trucks are held together with wire and then rope when the wire runs out. Spare parts are difficult to obtain and frequent breakdowns far from help are inevitable. Given this situation, everyone is eager to get their produce or passenger on a working truck and loading it is a mission. Stuff gets piled right up to the top of the sides of the truck bed. Filling every conceivable space with the maximum amount possible is the most important goal of the driver and his helper. Several relatives stand around to watch while they lean on sturdy canes. They comment on the efforts of the laboring workers like a Greek chorus, suggesting improvements and predicting doom. The bed of the truck is filled with crates placed so carefully together that they rival the Inca stonework in the Temple of the Sun. Bags of grain are piled on top of the crates, meticulously balanced, until they tower over the walls of the truck. The truck bows under this weight but retains just enough resiliency to hold the thirty-five women and children who climb up over the sides holding eighteen milk baskets. The men will clamber on just as the truck begins to move, searching for a comfortable place to sit that is not too precariously close to the edge of the truck, yet can allow a hasty exit should the need arise. From a distance, a fully loaded truck looks almost like a hot fudge sundae sprinkled with nuts on top.

That morning I spied an especially attractive place on the truck I was taking back to my teaching post near the border between Ethiopia and Somalia. It was a big wooden box placed next to the front side of the truck with nothing on top of it, although boxes and bags were piled on the three other sides. There was even enough room to tuck my legs over the side of the box so I wouldn't have to spend three hours with my feet curled under and no place to stretch them when they fell asleep. For some strange reason this particular spot had room to spare. I expected my friend from school, Subti, and several other travellers to sit down on the box next to me, but no one did. I had often longed for something to lean against on other truck rides, so I leaned back gratefully. However, my pleasure at having a back rest was quickly unraveled as this over-loaded omnibus disheveled its way over the rough terrain. There was nothing to prevent the persistent bumping of my back against the bare side of the truck as it bumped over the dirt track that only pretends to be a road in Somalia.

When we left the dusty field near the market, I wrapped myself in my big Somali cloak or *goa* to keep off the already burning sun and fashioned it into a hood about my face to keep out the blowing dust. Perched on the truck top near eight milk baskets called *dhills* and four fat women, I was tremendously glad, as always, when the truck began to creak forward. Immensely glad that the thing actually started and shocked that we were, in fact, moving.

Of course, progress doesn't last long. We must stop just outside town in order to pay for the ride. All the men jumped down and squatted in the shade of the truck. The women were left to gossip and roast in the desert sun. The driver counted his money and his passengers, haggled, joked, pissed, and prayed. At last we started to move again and the cooling wind against my face was marred only by the stinging dust in my eyes. By three or four this afternoon we would be lucky to reach Arabsiyo, where my house and school were located, thirty miles from here.

The sky is a large bowl overturned on the earth. It keeps everything in its place and ensures that the future will be much like the past. Despite the crumbling road and persistent but reassuring drone of the engine as it edged itself over the desert, the truck is not a quiet affair. The conversation is lively and continual. This is a social occasion and the Somali take full advantage, especially when a strange foreigner has joined the group.

"HiiYea," said a toothless but smiling old woman, pinching my arm. Her skin looked like an old paper bag rescued from the trash and smoothed out to be used again. "How can this woman be rich if she is so thin?" "Hadija," she said to her friend, "don't you think if she had some fat it would improve her looks." She ran her hand up my backbone to show that my bones protruded and she turned triumphantly to her audience having proved her point.

Hadija joined in the fun. She was large-boned and thin. Her dress was old and torn and the ragged edges of her petticoat hung beneath it. She had a strong voice and it boomed over the straining of the truck's motor. "Howa, Grandma, I doubt that more fat would do her any good. Who would marry anyone so ugly!" Everyone laughed and I rolled my eyes because I knew it was useless to argue the point.

"I wonder if she has a disease or was born with this dreadful white skin," the first murmured sympathetically stroking my arm.

"Mother, this is a very strange situation," teased Subti, who loved to play this game with unsuspecting nomads as we walked back to town from school. He liked to tease the women who watered their livestock at the wells we passed. "This woman is my sister," he said and waited to hear the gasp that always followed.

"*Wallahi!*" they both responded, loud enough to attract the attention of several other travellers.

"I was born like this, she like that, and we both had the very same mother. My hair is black, hers is red. My eyes are black, hers are blue. It was quite a shock to our poor mother, Allah protect her."

"*Wallahi!*" chorused the truck travellers.

"Your mother must have offended a *jinn*," replied the oldest woman, looking me over with obvious pity. "Only a spirit would play such a trick. Making a live person the same color as the devil!" She shook her head in sympathy and poked me gingerly to see if any of the terrible whiteness would come off my skin onto hers. To the Muslim believer, and in particular the Somali, the fire-born *jinn* are spirits, considered below the lowest of the angels. They can inspire, mislead, or even possess a man or woman who has faltered in the path of the faithful. Some *jinn* are good and others are not, but all serve to remind the faithful that the universe has its secrets hidden from the minds of men and women. Surely, my white skin, in contrast to my "brother" Subti's perfect dark features, must be the work of a mischievous *jinn*.

My red hair was not considered so terrible by the Somali, who are devout Muslims. In Muslim tradition, the angel Jibra'il, or Gabriel to Christians and Jews, is spoken of as a shining figure whose saffron hair is as luminous as the very stars in the night sky. Many Somali women use henna on their hair to beautify themselves. Men will use it on white beards for the same reason. It was agreed, however, by my sympathetic fellow travelers, that even my auburn hair would not help to dispel the ugly effect of my colorless skin. It was hopeless, no one would marry me. It was a good thing I had a job and could support myself.

An American friend had presented Subti with the gift of a necktie when I had introduced them during our trip to Hargeisa. Subti pulled the tie out from his little bundle and began to show it around to those on the truck.

"It's American," he said proudly. Everyone fingered the soft silk and admired the colors.

Finally, an intrepid soul risked the important question, "What does it do?"

"The American men wear it around their necks," replied Subti. He demonstrated how the tie was put on and I helped him to tie the slipknot. Everyone tried it on then, working the magical knot open and closed about their necks. Somali men wear a sort of skirt folded about the waist called a *ma'aweiss* and a short-sleeved shirt. Because of the relentless desert heat, the top shirt button is never closed. The men on the truck placed the tie about their necks as Subti and I instructed them, and sat wearing it looking rather silly and terribly uncomfortable. Again, the insistent questions began: "What does it do?"

Subti looked at me for help. "It doesn't do anything," I explained. "It is only for decoration." This was met with incredulous disbelief by a people who own nothing that is not useful. Possessions, for those who live in the desert, are only those items that are useful, and almost everything is used for many purposes.

The Somali have been nomadic travellers for centuries. They have learned how to move quickly and efficiently, because their lives and the livelihood of their families depends on quickly moving the herds of camels, cattle, and goats from the grasslands where they eat, to the wells in the dry season. For nomads, emphasis is on economy and simplicity in the design of their utilitarian possessions. This is appropriate to a people who move frequently and over long distances with their livestock in pursuit of pasture and water. Practical concerns override any others in the acquisition of clothing and anything else that must be carried. The stunning idea that the tie served no purpose whatsoever was totally unacceptable in this culture. The men refused to believe me, and Subti, although he knew it was true, was also at a loss to defend the concept.

The best example of a Somali article of clothing is the ubiquitous *goa*. This is a colorful cloth about the size of a sheet which everyone wears draped about the body like a cloak. The women have a smaller version called a *chalmut*. This was originally called a "Mericany" since the cloth was made in America. This piece of apparel rivals anything in the L. L. Bean catalog in its versatility and suitability for desert travel.

During a dusty trip on the back of a truck, one wraps the *goa* over one's head and mouth like a shawl. Thus the dust and dirt are kept out of your hair and other clothes as well as your mouth. If the day is fine and not dusty, you can sling the *goa* around your neck loosely like a scarf, where it will be out of the way. Should you stop for prayers, you can dip a corner of the *goa* in some water and use it as a washcloth to wash your hands and feet. If you are a heathen and don't pray, you can use it to wash your face and hands anyway. If the sun gets hot in the afternoon, you can wind it into a turban and use it to keep the sun off your head. Later, if it gets cool in the evening, you can wear it like a cape to keep warm. If you sold the goat you brought to market, you can tie the money in one corner of the *goa* and use it like a change purse. If the goat is unruly, you can tie him in the *goa* and keep him from wandering off. If you are trying to visit a girlfriend and her father is not too pleased about your visit, you can wrap yourself in the *goa* so only your eyes will show. Perhaps he will not know it is you slinking around the camp, trying to catch his daughter at the well. On trade trucks, when you are sitting on a hard box, you can fold it into a pillow and hope that it will cushion your bottom.

Despite all my efforts at explaining to my fellow travelers that the necktie had no earthly purpose they looked back at me in disbelief. Then, an enterprising young man pulled his *goa* up around his head. He put the necktie around his neck, over the *goa* and tightened it. This served to keep the cloth in place despite the blowing wind on the back of the truck and a resounding *"Saah"* or voiced assent came in unison from the truck voyagers. Western men must use the necktie to keep their *goas* securely on their heads when it is windy. They were obviously relieved to find that the strange item of apparel had a use, and I decided not to disabuse them of what they thought. I was being distracted at that point and was quite alarmed.

As the truck strained to cross the desert, I kept feeling hot air next to my left ankle. I assumed it was a little breeze wafting around the truck's cargo. However, the hot air puffs continued even when the truck was not moving. It was a sweltering morning and I was tired, too tired to bother with a little puff of hot air. I moved my foot closer to the box to avoid the draft. It stopped for a moment, but I soon felt an utterly strange sensation on my ankle that could not be ignored. It was the unmistakable wetness and roughness of a lick.

It is impossible to jump very far when ones legs are wedged between a wooden crate and bags of millet and the truck is pitching over another rough spot in the road. I tried to move my foot into the bags next to the box and doubled myself into a paper clip. I peered into the holes crudely cut into the top of the crate. As my eye slowly adjusted to the darkness within, I discerned the shape of a large beige animal. It was a lion, and he was licking my ankle.

There are some situations where one reacts different-ly from the way one would in other circumstances. It was very hot and dusty. I was very hot and tired. There was no place to move to and the truck was lurching down into a dry riverbed requiring me to hang on the side so I would not be pitched out. The lion was also very hot and tired. He looked up at me in abject misery. I felt exactly the same way. In addition to the pitching, rolling truck ride, I could tell that he and I shared a particular physical characteristic, we can't eat when we are upset. Knowing this, I knew without a doubt that I had nothing to fear from the poor beast. That is how I came to have an adventure while sitting on a lion.

The truck had continued its courageous labors all during the torpid and dusty afternoon. As we travelled, I realized that the lion was not about to move because he must have been shipped from the south, the only place a lion could still be found in Somalia. He was, most likely, on his way to the northern port of Berbera and I wondered if he would live to see it. He had been throwing up and was covered with ooze. He probably had licked my ankle in a desperate attempt to find some liquid. I was afraid he might die of dehydration. The Somali are quite cautious about cats, big and small. They do not keep pets other than their own herd animals. At last I understood why my cheerful companions had not taken a seat with me on the box. They would not sit anywhere near the lion, nor would they offer it food or water. The other travellers had known we had a feline passenger and kept a reserved distance. They had reserved that seat for me.

Without warning, several men on horses appeared out of the bush and blocked the road. They signaled for the driver to stop and shouted something in Somali that was unintelligible to me. The truck creaked to a halt and people began to climb out of the back of the truck. I took off my sandals, and stretched my legs out over the bags of grain. I was hoping for a peaceful moment alone in the truck while the Somali said their afternoon prayers. I had decided to try to give the lion something to drink.

After everyone left the truck, I slowly pried up a small section of the top of the box with my pocketknife. As I had suspected, the lion hardly moved despite the disturbance. I wet a corner of my goa with water and lowered it to the suffering animal. At first he seemed not to notice the water dripping into his panting mouth, then he took a few licks, but I feared it was too late.

Angry at the abuse of this poor miserable animal, I sat up and leaned out over the side of the truck to see what was going on. The driver was talking to one of the men on the horses. No one had even starting praying yet, but they were just standing in little groups talking quietly. I assumed the horsemen were relatives of the driver and were asking for a ride, or *quat*, or something. I took one of my dusty sandals and banged it on the side of the truck. *"Wham-a hii?"* I asked. "What is this?"

The horseman talking with the driver seemed surprised. He left the conversation he was having and rode over to the side of the truck. He looked at me, and my red hair blowing in the hot wind of the early afternoon. *"Muga-Ah,* what's your name?" he asked jauntily. Our eyes met boldly, since to look at a man directly is forbidden to Somali women.

"Jeanne," I replied. *"Muga i goo waa* Jeanne, I'm Jeanne." He returned my upturned gaze, and we appraised each other. He tightened his hands on the reins of his horse when his eyes suddenly recognized the shape of the lion, which had been revived by the water and began to stir in the open box I was sitting on. *"Muga-Ah?"* I asked him, enjoying his obvious surprise at the truck's cargo and his very handsome face. "Who are you?"

"Shifta, Wa Shifta," he replied quietly, looking deeply into my eyes. Then, for some strange reason, he handed me his hat. It was made of little brown burrs all stuck together to form the shape of a hat with a bill. I was looking at it when he signaled to his men. They rode off over the rolling hills into the desert and disappeared almost as quickly as they had come.

Subti, Hadija, Howa and the other travellers climbed back into the truck and the driver drove on without any further delays. This episode was discussed in great detail in highly animated conversation for the rest of the trip. Hadija's booming voice and wild gestulations echoed over the peaceful desert. She pointed at me repeatedly and the others nodded in voiced assent but I could not follow the Somali because it was much too fast and too excited. I was very tired from the exhausting heat and the rolling ride. I draped my *goa* over my head and dozed.

I was not home in Arabsiyo more that a few minutes

when Hadija appeared at my door with a man she said was her husband. "Osman," she said pointing to a thin, terribly tall, terribly black, terribly obseqious man who bowed frequently during her talk with me. I understood something about Osman guarding the house and tried to explain that I did not feel that I needed a guard. Hadija was not deterred by my efforts to say no and deposited the hapless man on my doorstep. I went inside and shut the door firmly determined not to have anything further to do with Osman.

Later that night, Abdillahi, the headmaster of my school, came to visit me with Subti and Abdul Kader, the two other teachers. He was one of the only Somali men I ever met who could be considered plump. He had a round belly and a pudgy face, and I liked him despite his often pompous attitude. He usually walked over to my house in the evening with Subti and Abdul Kader after they finished chewing *quat* for the day. He nodded to Osman who was still sitting on my doorstep and I hoped I could get him to tell Osman to go home.

"The town is talking and talking about you again, Jean," he said shaking his finger at me before I could say anything about my unwanted guard. Everyone had trouble pronouncing Jeanne but not Jean. "Do you Americans know what the Shifta warriors are?"

"No."

"These are bands of guerrillas who are fighting in the border dispute between the Somali and the Ethiopian governments. The British gave some of the Somali lands to the Ethiopians when they drew the maps of the two countries at the time of our independence in 1960. You were near the disputed territory today and some of these Shifta stopped the truck. They are renegades and were going to rob the truck. Didn't you see the guns they were carrying?" he asked incredulously, the white part of his eyes glowing in the light of the lamp.

"No." I never knew when to believe Abdillahi. I hadn't been looking for guns. I supposed they had been waving sticks.

"You were fearless, they are saying in town. You

banged on the side of the truck with your shoe and insulted the leader right to his face."

"I didn't mean to insult anybody. I was banging the dust off my sandal."

"Showing the bottom of the shoe is highly insulting to Muslims, don't you know that?"

"Oh." Another *faux pas*.

Then Abdillahi's eyes twinkled and he laughed. "This Shifta is from the interior. I think he had never seen a white woman closely before. He saw your white skin, and those blue eyes of yours, and your hair uncovered. He saw that you were not afraid of him, and then he saw that you were sitting on a lion. He was worried that you might be the actual devil herself and has run back into Ethiopia, the hyena." Abdillahi was obviously pleased with himself for figuring out what happened during my encounter with the Shifta.

"That's not what happened at all," interrupted Subti who never minded contradicting Abdillahi. "There is a story in the Quran about Mohammed and a prostitute at a well. She had seen a dog who was very thirsty but could not draw any water up from the well. She dipped her shoe into the water and gave it to the dog. Mohammed said that all her sins would be forgiven because of her kindness."

"Jean," he continued with a little smile, "everyone thinks you are a prostitute because you are not closed (infibulated). When the Shifta asked who was sitting on the truck, the driver told him it was the American prostitute living in Arabsiyo. That Shifta remembered the story from the Qur'aan when he saw that you were giving water to the lion. I think he decided not to rob the truck for fear of offending Allah. He thought you brought a message from God."

In Somalia there is never one version of an event, there are always at least three that are endlessly discussed and reconsidered. This was no exception. "I heard this in town," said Abdul Kader who had not been on the truck. "The Shifta went up to the truck and saw this very strange woman. He wanted to know who this is. 'Jean, that's Jean,' everyone from the truck told him. He thought the people were telling him that it was a *jinn*. He didn't believe it until he went up to see this spirit and you said it yourself, 'I'm Jean,' you told him, everyone heard it. Then he got scared since everyone is telling him there is a *jinn* on the truck, including the *jinn*. He left to protect his men from this bad truck spirit."

"Anyway," Abdillahi said, to regain control of the situation, "I'm glad that you will have a night watchman, you get into much trouble."

"But Abdillahi, I don't want a watchman," I started to tell him, but he interrupted me and I knew from experience that it was useless for me to continue.

"Hadija came to my house and spoke with me about her husband, Osman Tuuk. I already agreed that he would be a good watchman for you. You should pay him twenty-five shillings a week."

"Doesn't *tuuk* mean thief?" I asked, incredulous that the man proposed as my guard would be called Osman the Thief.

"He sells things to foreigners," Abdillahi retorted as if that explained anything. I tried to insist that I really did not feel afraid, did not want a watchman, and resented not even being consulted, but Abdillahi dismissed me with a wave of his hand as if I were a naughty schoolboy. His eyes rested on the new flashlight I had just purchased in Hargeisa that morning. "I will need this torch to patrol the town tonight in case the Shifta decide to come back. Thank you for the gift," he said, taking the flashlight from my table. "I think you should write a letter to your father and tell him what good care I am taking of you here in Somalia. He should send me a present."

"Taking care of what?" I asked in total exasperation. This was the second flashlight that Abdillahi had taken.

"I'm seeing that no one is fucking you."

"Abdillahi," I said, incredulous at his assumption, "that is a very rude word in my language." Subti shook his head and rolled his eyes behind Abdillahi's back. Abdul Kader leaned forward and looked as if he hoped I would explain a little more about this American fucking.

"That's the problem with your language," Abdillahi retorted. "You have only this one word in English, fucking. In my language we have so many words I can talk for days about fucking."

Abdillahi left taking Subti, Abdul Kader, and my new flashlight with him. He and Osman the Thief had a long conversation outside the door, it opened, and Osman moved inside the house. He squatted on a mat in the courtyard and looked at me with a mixture of fear and loathing. I was furious, I wondered how Osman could watch the house from the inside. However, it was too late to argue the point with Abdillahi, I could see the three of them walking through the dark streets outside my house, safe in the little circle of light from my flashlight. Abdillahi was still loudly discussing the day's events with Subti and Abdul Kader. He wanted my flashlight and he wanted to boss everyone around and feel important and powerful. He did not want the Shifta hat, which I still have and will always treasure.

I wondered if I would ever be able to understand what was happening around me. I seemed to miss most of whatever was going on. Reality seemed fluid: somehow the laws of gravity had been suspended in Africa. Things were not what they seemed before, during, or after events. I realized with some satisfaction that even if I did not understand, I was becoming part of the folklore of the village. The story of Jeanne and the Shifta would be told over and over again. The tale would define me and would be used to help others understand the strange American woman who lived so far away from her father and his people. This is how those who live in an oral society learn and grow. I realized that I would never really understand the people I met until I knew their stories, until I could see the world from inside thier hearts and minds. I needed to tell the stories as they would, to see me as they did. To the Somalis who knew me I was a helpless frightened childlike creature, unaware of her own great power to change the couse of events in this little village. Perhaps I really was a *jinn* with the power to torment, confuse, and mislead the faithful follows of Islam.

I have often reflected on the handsome Shifta and why

he decided not to rob the truck. I wonder if in the brief moment we shared, he saw that I was a renegade, like he was. I had obviously left my family and had gone off in search of a greater adventure, alone, and outside the reach of my own people. He and I were both wild enough to have insisted on doing something very dangerous. I lived alone in Africa in the name of world understanding, he was fighting for the re-unification of the Somali people. We were both young, idealistic, and adventurous. I would like to think that he gave me his Shifta hat not because he feared that I was a *jinn* or the devil, but because he saw that in my own way, I too was a Shifta warrior. I hope that is the way he tells the story to his children and his clansmen.

Hearts of Stone

*Time and trouble will tame
an advanced young woman,
but an advanced old woman
is uncontrollable by any
earthly force.*

—Dorothy L. Sayers

All Somali girls have their clitoris
and the lips of the minor labia cut off
prior to puberty. During this operation,
the remaining flesh is stitched together
so that the wound will heal tightly
closed. This is called infibulation and is
done to ensure that intercourse prior to
marriage is impossible. The practice of
female circumcision is widespread
among Muslims throughout the world.
Some claim that it is prescribed in the
Hadith, the collection of traditions
which record how the Prophet
Mohammed practiced the Quran in his
daily life, but the Hadith contains no
written injunction regarding female circumcision.

I knew about this practice from my reading about Somalia, however I could not understand why mothers would allow their daughters to be mutilated in this way until I heard Asha's story. I met her at a wedding my first night in Arabsiyo and visited her whenever I was in Hargeisa. She also came out to Arabsiyo frequently to visit her family and we became good friends. She had lived in London and understood more than anyone else the difficulties I encountered in my efforts to understand the Somali way of life because of her own troubles with the British.

Asha was not married but she was so lovely that I knew it would only be a little while before some wonderful man would claim her. The afternoons I spent with her were some of the happiest times I spent in Somalia. She was intelligent as well as elegant and I learned a great deal from her about being a woman. She introduced me to many of her friends - women like her who were educated, sophisticated, and fascinating. I first met Asha on the wedding night of her friend Assia who was being married to a man much older than she. She left me that night to be with Assia during the opening of the infibulation by the Midgaan woman. Later Asha introduced me to Assia so that I could talk with her about her wedding night and hear the story of her arranged marriage. I always missed Asha when she went back to Hargeisa and waited eagerly for her next visit. Asha was a wonderful teacher and she helped me to understand the reasons she accepted her own infibulation.

Asha's Story

I was born in the Northern region of Somalia while it was still a British protectorate. My grandfather admired the British and he sent my father, Mohammed Abdi, to England to be educated. Grandfather felt that the future of Africans would be determined by how well they understood the British. When my father returned to Somalia, his marriage to my mother was arranged by the two clans. Eventually, my father helped to negotiate the terms of Somali independence from Great Britain and Italy. He was invited to continue his political work in the Somali Embassy in London by the new government.

I think I was about six when he brought my mother, my baby sister and I to live with him in London. I adored my father. He was very tall even for a Somali, and had light-colored skin like mine. He had a special name for me different from Asha, the name my mother gave me. Then he called me Faadumo after the sister of the Prophet Mohammed. "Faadumo was a very wise and powerful woman, she led her people after her brother's death. You should be a leader to your own people," he said.

He had an angular face which softened when he laughed and he always had a smile and a story for me. My favorite was Zobeide from the *Tales of a Thousand and One Nights*. "Zobeide sailed away from her own country," he began. "She came to a harbor but found the streets of the town strangely silent and empty. She could not find anyone anywhere."

"Not a single person in the whole town!" I would wonder. I had never been entirely alone in my whole life. It was hard to imagine what it would be like. Like all Somali babies I had been carried in a sling on my mother's soft back, or by her sisters, or by my cousins. We ate together and slept cuddled together on a large mat covered with warm cloths. No one in my family was ever alone. "Were the people out in the interior watching the goats?" I asked.

"No, Faadumo, there wasn't anyone watching the goats, or the camels, or the sheep," he explained. "Zobeide was all alone. Finally she came to a magnificent palace. There were many riches strewn about in every room, but Zobeide still could not find another living soul. She became lost and finally fell asleep, exhausted from her long journey. At midnight she was awakened by the sound of someone praying. The familiar words of the Quran were sweet music to her poor lonely ears and she followed the sound. Soon she found a young man praying on a Muslim prayer mat. He was overjoyed to see her, a fellow Muslim. He explained that he was the prince of the city and the only person left.

All of the other inhabitants of the city had been fire wor-
shipers. When the one true God, Allah, asked them to worship Him, they had all refused."

"Why didn't they want to worship Allah?" I asked.

"Faadumo, they felt that they were so rich they didn't
need God. They were stone-hearted to his request to love
him and to follow the five pillars of Islam. Eventually their
bodies as well as their hearts turned to stone. Only the
prince did not turn to stone because he was a faithful
Muslim."

I loved that story because I felt like Zobeide. I had also
journeyed to a strange place filled with many riches and
people who were not Muslim. It is an incredible experience
for a child to leave a two-room whitewashed house without
plumbing or electricity in Somalia and come to London.

When we got off the plane at Heathrow Airport, I
thought the sun must stay close to Somalia and far away
from England because it was so grey and cold. My shadow
had been a daily playmate in the warm and peaceful desert.
My father took my hand and led us through a blur of legs,
odd smells, floors that moved, doors that whirled, and the
total absence of sheep and goats. I had never seen so many
people and such unhappy faces. This was not like the empty
city that Zobeide had discovered on her travels. I hoped my
father would never, ever, let go of my hand. I looked out of
the big windows at the terminal and saw other buildings.
They were bigger than anything I had ever seen at home and
I thought one must be Hempstead where we would live,
another must be London where my father would go to work.

"Look at that, *Hooyo*, Mother," I said, pointing at some
women walking by. I was surprised to see that the heels on
their shoes were very tall and thin. "How can they walk
with their heels up on the air? Doesn't it hurt their feet?" I
really wanted to know about these shoes.

"Those are high heel shoes," replied my mother.

"Do the English ladies have to wear them?" I asked,
worried that I would have to wear shoes like that as well.

"The British women wear them to make themselves
more beautiful."

"But, *Hooyo*, don't they hurt?" I continued, glad I had my comfortable brown sandals. The Midgaan shoemaker had traced my feet onto a piece of paper and made sandals especially for me, exactly my size.

"I think they must," said my mother laughing at these silly women. My mother was elegant and poised. Her delicate features were balanced by strong, intelligent eyes. She moved slowly and seemed to float when she walked. She was always telling me; "Slow down and walk like a camel, Asha." I wondered why these English women would do something painful in order to make themselves beautiful.

People were eating things right out in front of everyone, which shocked me. No Somali, no matter how poor, would be so unclean. "*Aba*, what are they eating?" I wanted to know.

"Hot dogs," he replied and I dropped my father's hand to watch in amazement. English people ate dogs! I couldn't believe it. I fervently hoped that we would be able to buy some goats in the market and would not have to eat dog meat like the British.

When we arrived at the house my father had arranged for us, he took us through all the rooms. In the kitchen he turned on the faucet and showed us how to make the water hot or cold. My sister and I played in the stream of water and were astonished that it could flow out of the pipe so quickly. Then my father told us the biggest surprise.

"This water will never stop," he said. I thought he must be teasing. Surely even the British weren't rich enough to have so much water that it would never stop.

"There are pipes like this in Mogadishu," said my mother.

"Yes," he answered, "but, that's just sea water from the ocean. This is fresh water you can drink right now."

"At my house in Hargeisa the water boy, or *biouli*, brought water every other day. Our precious water came from deep wells located in the *tuug* or dry river bed outside of town. The *biouli* had a donkey with two large square tins strapped on either side. He would climb up a ladder on the side of our house, carrying a tin on his back, and pour the water into one of two large black tanks. We used one tank one day, the other the next. Parasites die in still water within 24 hours so we alternated using the tanks to be sure that the water was not infected. During the day, the water in the tanks would heat up in the sun. It would be warm enough for a bath in our big flat washbasin in the afternoon. Often I had climbed up the ladder for my mother, to see how much water was left. The idea of a pipe endlessly filled with water was very difficult for any child coming from the desert to understand.

"Leave the water on all night!" I shouted. I wanted to see when it would stop.

"That would be wasteful," he said, turning the faucet off. "But, *Habibe*, you can turn it on and off as many times as you want to. The water will always come out." I did just that. Every time I passed a faucet I would turn it on just to see and, sure enough, water always came pouring out. I waited for the wonderful water man who had donkeys that could carry that much water, but he never came.

There were cars and buses on every street and they never seemed to stop either. I wondered where all these people were going and where we would be able to keep our goats. All the streets were paved so there wasn't anything for the goats to eat. Everyone wore colorful clothes, shoes with strings, and big coats with buttons. My favorite things were umbrellas. They were like porcupines because they could open right up with great big spikes.

The shops were filled with more food than I had ever seen together in one place and had greater variety than I ever knew existed. No wonder there isn't much food in Somalia, I thought, the British have kept it all for themselves. For a long time I thought the shops were all closed because there was no way I could see to get in. In Somalia the shutters in front of the shop are up when it is opened and down when it is closed. These doors were always closed. I could see people inside and imagined that the British would not tell us Somalis how to get in. Eventually I realized that the shop doors were not locked, and the shops were open even when the doors were closed. I found out that the British had to live like this because of the cold weather. In my country the weather is warm most of the time and the shopkeepers do not have to close themselves away from the daylight and the people. It seemed as though Somalia was open and England was all closed up.

The British clerks were not friendly or helpful to me. They acted suspicious when I went into the shops and they made me feel as though I were dirty or something by the way they were always watching me.

"What do you want?" they would say as they leaned on the counter and frowned at me.

Nothing from people who eat dog meat, I thought to myself. I could understand the tone and the look long before I was confident enough to answer in English. I would point at the bread or oranges my mother asked me to buy and put my money on the counter. I thought that the British had hearts of stone. They didn't smile and tease like the people I knew in the shops back in Hargeisa. They never offered a special treat for a little girl. They were not Muslim, and they actually ate dogs and even pigs which are forbidden in the Quran. They worshiped Jesus as if he were a God even though he was a really only a prophet just like Moses and Mohammed. I supposed they thought they didn't need Allah because they were so rich. This made me very angry and I hoped that those disapproving white faces would soon turn to stone like the people in the story of Zobeide.

My father taught me how to pray and told me that turning to Allah in prayer is the simplest and best way of gaining His protection. I felt joined with my cousins and family back home during the *salat* or worship. In my houses in Somalia and in England we turned our bodies toward Mecca and our hearts to God five times a day. Reciting the Quran drew me close to my distant clan, more precious to me than the never ending water in my new home. My father taught me the thirteen *arkan* or essentials which dictate exactly what we say and do when we pray.

Muslims begin by standing and facing Mecca while we recite the opening Sura:

"In the name of Allah, the Beneficent, the Merciful.

Praise be to Allah, Lord of the Worlds."

Then we bow from the waist, reciting praise to God. This is followed by the *sujad* when we kneel and touch our foreheads to the ground while we say a prayer of submission. More bowing and kneeling follow. I never felt like a stranger while praying, I knew that there were thousands of others who were praying exactly like me: Muslims faithful to Allah. Like Zobeide, whenever I met another Muslim in this strange country, I felt a very special connection to this person because of our religion.

My father did not allow us to return to Somalia to visit our families when my sisters and I were growing up because he did not want us to be infibulated. He considered it primitive and unnecessary. Although he was deeply religious, he did not agree with the Somali custom of female circumcision and forbade my mother to have this done to his daughters.

She argued long and bitterly with him that we would be considered whores by our own countrymen.

"We will not be able to find suitable husbands for our daughters if they are left open," she argued. "Anybody could marry Asha but then turn right around and divorce her the next day. People would say she deserved it." Traditional Somalis believe that uncircumcised women are driven to acts of unfaithfulness by an uncontrollable sex drive caused by the clitoris. "No decent family would approve of marriage to such a woman," my mother continued. "Just look at these British girls kissing and holding hands with boys all over the place! Is that what you want for your daughters? Everyone at home will have enough questions because the girls grew up in a non-Muslim country. Let's not make it worse by ignoring our traditions."

My father answered her with the same argument every time the subject came up. "These are superstitions held by uneducated people who live in the desert. They know very little of the modern world."

"Mohammed, I will take the girls to Saudi Arabia where they can be circumcised by a doctor in a hospital," my mother countered.

"Hebo, how can women experience any pleasure in sex with mutilated bodies? The Quran says nothing about cutting off little girls' genitals," he said. "There is no reason for this to be done." Finally he just told her, "I will not have my daughters mutilated because of a barbaric custom. I forbid you to have this done."

"If you stop a tradition, it will make God angry." She answered with a Somali proverb, but he did not change his mind.

Eventually the subject was no longer discussed, but I knew from the look on my mother's face that it was not finished. She kept the silence of strength, not of resignation. She taught us the poem:

The wife who nags is like
Satan himself.
Always be sensitive, walk prudently,
and speak slowly.
Mind your neighbor and language,
for decency is noble.

I used to lie in bed listening for the even breathing that came when my sister had fallen asleep. I would touch myself and wonder what they cut. How does it feel to be sewn together? It did seem purer, less tempting with little to explore, nothing but flat skin instead of my moist self with ridges. I washed and washed in the morning afraid that someone would smell my fingers and know what I had touched in the night.

My mother said that in the old days the cutting was done with a sharpened stone or a piece of glass. "Now," she said, "we are more modern, and the Midgaan women use a razor blade or a sharp knife. When I was a child the young girls were not allowed to cry or they would not have any presents. "Today," she added, "there are many presents even when a weak girl cries." I wondered if I would have been a strong girl, or a weak girl who cried. I knew my sister would be weak and cry.

"In the old days," she told us, "the nomads would use the sharp thorn of the golol tree to close up the incision. Now the girls are stitched carefully together with a proper needle." My mother believed that the process had been harsh at one time, but that things had changed. She did not convince my father that things had changed. I was grateful that I did not live in the old days, and still afraid of the present.

My mother said that the cutting is done by Midgaan women who are very skilled. The Midgaans are considered a lower class in Somalia because they do not trace their lineage to the prophet Mohammed like noble Somalis. My mother's sister Halimo came to visit us once in London. She told us a story about the Midgaans.

"A woman once had two husbands. She slept with one during the day and the other at night. Both of her husbands died suddenly and she gave birth to a posthumous baby of uncertain parentage. The child was possessed by a demon and went to live in the bush. He was found and rescued by a Somali and became the first Midgaan."

The Midgaans engage in activities considered unclean by many Muslims. The men make shoes, and women do the ritual infibulation. To show the bottom of the shoe to someone is a grave insult. For a man to touch a woman's vagina except during intercourse is ritually impure and the faithful must wash again before praying.

Gradually I learned to speak English at school. I liked languages and became fluent in Arabic and French as well as English. My father was proud of my academic success, and I worked even harder to win one of his increasingly rare smiles.

Over the years as I grew older, I started to feel as if I could be both Somali and British. Yet, I was often reminded that I would never be accepted by the British. I remember very vividly what happened the first day that I attended intermediate school. The teacher called me up to her desk in front of everyone.

"This is Ashe and we are lucky to have her with us because she comes from darkest Africa," she said. She had fat hanging from her arms and red splotches on her white face. The Somalis believe that fat women are beautiful, but as I studied this teacher's many chins, I thought that this is not true for white people.

I said, "My name is Asha," because I couldn't think how else to answer her. I thought: Darkest Africa? Africa is sunny and light, London is dark. Later I read about Gandhi. Once someone in Parliament had remarked to him, "I hear in your country they worship the sun." He had replied, "You would too if you ever saw it." I waited to be able to use that remark, but I never did.

In history class we studied about Sir Richard Burton. The teacher said he discovered East Africa. I sat at my desk with my cheeks burning. How could he discover something when there were lots of people who already lived there? He should have just asked.

As I grew older I felt like I lived in two worlds in London. At my school, and with my father, I marveled at the British. How free they were! It seemed they would say or do just about anything. At home, I gradually stopped talking about my girlfriends, or the boys who flirted with me. Mother did not go out, did not have British friends and disapproved of almost everything I told her. I learned to ask to go out when my father was home. He often took my part.

"I want to go with the girls to a soccer game."

"Soccer? Asha, I really don't think that's appropriate for a young girl. You will miss the evening prayers."

"Mother, the only thing you think is appropriate for me to do is stay home. Praying five times a day is too much, you can't do anything else."

"Faadumo," said my father, "Allah originally commanded Mohammed and the faithful to pray fifty times a day. Moses told him to go back up to God and complain that it was too much. That's why we only have to pray five times a day."

"I've asked fifty times to go out with my friends," I replied. "Even Allah gave in to Mohammed. Why don't you ever give in to me?"

My father understood my two worlds, he lived a dual life too. Usually he laughed and said, "Go ahead to the soccer game."

My mother stayed in the kitchen and cooked or

worked on her embroidery, drinking sweet spiced tea she made with cardamom. She did not go out or have friends. She loved to dance and taught us many dances in the dark afternoons. She played the tambourine and we had tapes of Somali songs. My mother was waiting to go back to Somalia, to be with her family again. I was afraid to be free and open like the British, afraid to be like my mother who had been sewn shut.

I was eighteen, a woman long past the age of infibulation, when my father was recalled from the foreign service and we returned to live in Hargeisa. We did not have endless water running out of our faucets, but we had the funny little water man. He came to our house every other day and always had a toothless smile and gentle donkeys. We did not have toilet bowls filled with water to flush. Our house, like most of the others in the Northern towns of Somalia, had a "long drop." This was a very deep hole with a keyhole shaped opening at the top. You squat over the hole with your feet positioned on the sides of the keyhole. Frankly, I think it is much cleaner and more comfortable that the *loos* in London. Our house had two front rooms separated by an entrance corridor. It had an inner courtyard and the long drop and a cooking shed at the rear of the courtyard. There were no glass windows, no carpets, or brass handles. Still, it was a functional house, well suited to a warm climate with little rain.

Soon after we returned, my grandfather suggested that my father take a second wife. I was not surprised at the suggestion since my father had no sons by my mother. I was shocked at how quickly my father agreed to marry a silly village girl. She was only a little older than me and scurried around like a servant, waiting on my father as if he were a God or something. My father lived half of the week with my mother and the other half with this second wife. On their wedding night she was cut open so he could enter her body. I was jealous and I hoped it hurt her. Under Muslim law a man can have up to four wives so long as all are treated equally, but I had not expected this from my father. Coming home to Somalia was just as difficult as learning to live in

London had been. Odd things happened that I did not understand at first. One day an old woman with tattered clothes and a face like bark stood outside the house, shouting for someone to come out. I opened the door to tell her to go away.

"Give me your slip," she said. "mine is old and torn and you are rich, kinswoman."

"Get out of here," I said. "What makes you think I am so rich? I only have one slip, if I give it to you I won't have any."

"Is this how you treat members of your own clan, your own kinswoman? Go back to England." She spit at me and shuffled off on bare feet with leather amulets on her arms and around her neck to keep the devil away.

I felt different from my family and friends. All my cousins wanted to talk about was getting married, their bride price, how many children they wanted. They wondered aloud about my problem. I slowly realized that not being circumcised was a very grave concern. It was not considered old fashioned in Hargeisa, it was an absolute requirement for marriage. I had been the only African in my class in England. Now I was the only "open" girl in all of Somalia. I needed my father's strength and understanding, but he was involved with this new wife, and did not spend any time with me.

Early one morning I went to the market to see what was fresh and buy food for our noon meal. First I stopped at the Hajji Aden's shop where I would buy little packages of spices wrapped in newspaper, and tea, weighed on the little scale with an ancient quarter pound and wrapped into a little paper cone. Hajji had sunken cheekbones but warm eyes. He was a direct relative and also a friend of my grandfather. He was protective of me, and silenced the other men in his shop with a look. Hajji called his young son to take my money. The little boy was sitting on a burlap sack behind the counter and eating his breakfast of pancakes and goat milk. He reached up on tiptoe to take the shilling and put it into the tin can that served as a cash register. Hajji would never touch me or even the money I held because he had washed that morning in preparation for his daily prayers. Water is precious in the desert and he would have to wash again if he came into contact with me. I was ritually impure, like all children who have not yet been circumcised. Until the circumcision is done, the child is considered *haram*, unlawful, unclean, and cannot prepare food or touch a man who is in a state of ritual purity.

I hurried on into the open air market, where things were more relaxed. There, I might buy a cut of the goat meat hanging on a hook and covered with flies. Animals cannot be eaten if they die on their own, they must be properly slaughtered. After slitting the animal's throat the butcher will hang the goat on a hook to drain the blood since blood is also considered ritually impure. I bought several cones of rice and some lemons and oranges from the gardens in Arabsiyo. The market was a cheerful place, everyone teased each other, and haggled over the prices.

"Mother, how much are these lemons?"

"They are fresh this morning, three gumbos each," said the placid, smiling woman, sitting on the ground behind her basket of lemons. She had carried the basket on her head for many miles from the orchards to sell in the market.

"Give me two lemons for three *gumbos*."

"Daughter, these are large lemons, Allah be praised."

"*Hiyea*, they are big. How about two lemons for four *gumbos*?"

"Two lemons, five *gumbos*," she said. She cocked her head to the side, and smiled so that the deep wrinkles in her face stood out like the cracks in the earth during a drought. I was happy to pay this sweet woman. "O, what a beauty you are, Allah be praised," she said, touching my hands and giving me a gentle squeeze when I held out the money to her gnarled fingers.

I was walking back from the market with goat meat, spices, and rice, when I felt a stone hit my back. I turned and saw two boys hiding at the side of a neighboring house. One picked up another stone from the ground and boldly threw it right at me. "Whore! Whore!" they shouted and ran off laughing. Other people watched and did nothing. Hot tears of embarrassment and anger burned my cheeks. I was tempted to drop my basket and catch those monsters but I saw my mother watching me, her taut face framed in the blue shutters of the window.

Not long after that, when my father was away with his second wife, a car pulled up in front of our house in the middle of the night. People I did not know, but who were addressed by name by my mother, took my two sisters and me from our beds and wrapped us in the sheets. Screaming, I looked up to see my mother's frightened face framed in the same window as they carried us from the house. Neighbors gathered to observe, but stood silently and did not stop the car from speeding away through the dusty streets of Hargeisa and out into the night.

I was terrified. I knew immediately why we had been kidnapped. Our relatives were appalled that we had never been infibulated. They were taking us to the interior where my father would not be able to find us. They would see that the operation was done, and bring us back when it was over.

Not having been circumcised had been normal in London, I could forget all about it, but I was back home in Somalia again. I was panicked about the cutting, but was also afraid to be the only woman in town who was not infibulated. I was ritually impure, like the little children, and could not even be touched by devout Muslim men. Already there was talk and looks from the men and boys. I had been stoned and called a whore. I could see what was behind their eyes even when I could not hear the comments.

I did not want to be so different from everyone else. I wanted to be married, to have children and a home of my own, I wanted to be accepted. I had always been an outsider in London and I did not want to be alien in my own country. The shopkeepers in Hargeisa, like those in London, looked at me as though I was dirty, they considered me unlawful, unclean. Only circumcision makes a person *halal*, or lawful for religious instruction or marriage.

When we finally stopped, I was surprised that my

grandmother was one of the women who came to take us from the car. The women ululated into the starry night filling the spaces between the stars with the high-pitched controlled warble. With great joy they had come to claim their kin and make them into real Somali women.

"My father will kill you if you do this!" I shouted at my grandmother but I couldn't control my voice which shook with fear and rage. I could feel hot urine running down my legs.

"*Enshallah*," she answered calmly. 'If God wills.' Her eyes were white with cataracts but I knew she could see what was important.

The conical hut was built of woven mats draped over the long elastic branch of the acacia tree. Inside, a small brazier was burning with charcoal. A woman pounded myrrh, a resin she had gathered from the thorny golol tree, and tossed it into the coals. It filled the air with sweet smelling smoke, and my eyes filled with hot tears. I was dragged onto a straw mat covered with cloth. My grandmother held my head up so I could see what was happening and she began to sing with the women: "Now you are strong and beautiful, now you have become a woman."

Someone pulled my clothing up around my waist, and other strong hands grabbed my legs and pulled them apart despite my struggle. Suddenly the Midgaan entered the circle of women who surrounded me and positioned herself between my legs. She was a large woman, big boned and muscular. Her face was not Somali, she had a flat nose and big lips.

She paused as if waiting for permission to begin and I saw my sister watching in terror. Women were holding their daughter's faces up so they would watch. I tried not to scream for her sake as the Midgaan placed her warm hands between my legs and pulled my clitoris up and away from my vagina. She cut the clitoris off swiftly using a razor blade with a careful, steady hand. I was determined not to cry out, not to give in, but when she continued cutting and cutting, I heard my own screaming right over the intense sound of the women's continual ululation. After an agony of time, she stopped and sat back on her heels to watch. Gentle hands washed the wound with a mixture of oil of myrrh and water to cleanse it and prevent inflammation.

I had only begun to sense the pulsing, throbbing fire between my legs, when she began again. This time she stitched the outer lips of my vagina together to close the wound. She left only a small opening for urine and menstrual blood.

My legs were bound together by long strips of cloth to prevent any separation of the wound. I would only be able to hop with my legs bound together for several weeks. I watched as the women turned to my sister, Ibado. She appeared slightly calmer, despite my screaming. Her eyes were large and they seemed to fill up her entire face, but she did not struggle and fight. Maybe imagining the cutting is worse than it is to see it.

Kind women who understood, supported my throbbing body as I was moved to a straw mat and placed on cushions and pillows. Henna-dyed hands held sweet spiced tea to my lips. "Leave me alone," I said, knowing that it would be excruciating to urinate. My grandmother held me until I was too tired to cry any longer. She smelled of wood smoke and milk and her hands were very wrinkled yet supple as she caressed me over and over. If pain and work had etched the lines, then love had softened them. She smiled proudly as she slipped two gold bracelets onto my wrist. They caught the flickering flames of the little charcoal fire and sparkled in the flickering light. A gift of gold means love. I remember that long night very well. I remember that I had never felt so much pain, but I have never felt so very wanted.

I waited for my father, but he never came. I couldn't believe it. A few days later we were driven back to Hargeisa. My father was angry and he did not come back to my mother's house for a long time.

"You allowed this to happen," he shouted at my mother.

"It was *your* mother who did this, not mine," she answered him. "He who refuses to accept the knowledge of old women will lose his children," she said, looking steadily into his face. If she couldn't quote the Quran a proverb would do.

After that, my father's visits became very formal, we would sit in a circle and he would ask each one to speak with him in turn. My sisters and I would tell him about our school work or other activities with our eyes to the floor.

"Father, I need a new notebook for school."

"Father, I want to go to the Sheik's tomb for his birthday celebration."

I knew never to look directly into his face, never to have our eyes meet, never to speak unless spoken to. I guess I never saw my father again, not as I knew him in London. Now that I have been infibulated I am a proper Somali woman, and I have many prospects for a good marriage. However, when I touch myself in the stillness of the Somali night, I feel the scarred skin between my legs. I remember Zobeide and the faithful Muslim prince whose family and friends turned to stone. I am accepted by my family and friends, but I feel like a piece of my body has turned to stone. *Enshallah* it will not always be like this.

Osman the Thief

*If once pride held my head
erect, now my back is bent;
However much manliness
men claim,
time will grind them . . . .*
—*Somali Gabay*
by Salaan Arrabey

A few months after his wife Hadija got him a job as a guard, Osman heard his name being called softly by his mistress. It was a tone of voice he had never heard her use before. It sounded like the little bleat of a baby goat that is lost and stalked by a predator. It does not want to betray its location, but it desperately wants help.

It was late and so Osman had been dozing in the little room at the back of the house. He was the night watchman for this strange American woman who lived alone. Hadija had seen how little Americans can do for themselves and realized she needed someone to protect her.

What a clever wife he had! She had suggested Osman as a guard to the headmaster of the school at which the American was teaching. Abdillahi, the headmaster, had agreed and Osman had started guarding her that very night. He often wondered if he was guarding her from those in the village or guarding the villagers from the trouble she could cause.

Osman heard his mistress' urgent little bleat again through his dreaming, "Osman." It was late, he could see the light from the lamps in his mistress' big room, the moon had almost set. She had been working there at her table when he went to the back of the house. Osman eased his old bones out of the bed and quietly came across the courtyard in the center of the house. Through the open door leading into the front room of the house from the inner court, Osman could see his mistress' white cat playing with something on the floor. Osman did not like cats, and he couldn't understand why the boss would actually have such a dirty, useless creature living with her in the house. She had discovered it wandering near the garbage pile behind the market place one day and actually picked the filthy flea-infested thing up with her bare hands and brought it right into the house. She could have purchased fine goats or camels if she wanted some animals, they are clean and useful because they give milk and meat. It was bad enough working for an unclean infidel without having to endure this useless animal rubbing against his leg.

The cat had an insect of some sort and was batting it back and forth with its paws. Whatever had frightened his mistress had not disturbed the cat's play, which was odd. Even a worthless cat can smell and sense a stranger, or danger. The cat played on in the quiet room, totally involved in its game. It was oblivious to whatever concerned the mistress.

Osman was standing silently in the courtyard, watching through the doorway, and trying to sense what was the matter, when the American woman called again. "Osman." She could have been saying, hello, the tone of her voice was so mild. Her voice floated, laced with fear, out into the courtyard and circulated inside his head. The vocalization of fear being purposely hidden was clear to Osman.

Osman moved again to a position a little closer to the open door and cautiously stood outside, waiting and ready to act. His mistress was sitting with her bare feet tucked up underneath her on the chair. She was leaning on her papers and watching the cat play on the floor. She sensed that Osman was just outside and when she looked up at him, her eyes were pleading for him to do something.

Then he saw it! The cat had a scorpion and was playing with it. It was a tiny scorpion about two inches long and they are the most deadly. It had its killing tail curled up like the half moon over its back, and was trying to get into position to strike the stupid cat. The cat played on with its demonic toy, unaware of its imminent demise. Suddenly Osman understood, his mistress was barefoot, she did not dare try to kill the scorpion, or even push it out of the way. If she had distracted the cat with any sound of alarm, its momentary inattention would have given the scorpion an opportunity to land a deadly strike. She had called to him softly, so as not to disturb this lethal game in any way.

Osman stepped on the little killer, and crushed it beneath his shoe. The cat still had one paw raised for another little pat, and stood there dumbly, but the game was over. The American scooped that cat up off the floor and began to cry. She was a strange looking woman, short with white skin and blue eyes so bright they reflected the noon sky. Many people in town thought she was either a devil or a *jinn*. Her white skin became red and blotchy when she cried. It never ceased to amaze Osman, skin changing color like that.

"Oh Osman, how did you come so quietly?" she exclaimed. "I was afraid if I distracted the cat, she would be stung by the scorpion and die. Thank you, thank you, Osman," she said, holding the worthless bit of filthy fur right up next to her face.

The cat stared at Osman in anger and disbelief, a fine thanks for saving its life. The mutual dislike between the two of them increased.

These Americans are strange, Osman thought back in his room. Why would anyone keep such trouble in the house? There was just no making sense of these foreigners. The cat did nothing except sleep, eat, carry fleas, hiss at everybody, and piss. What a filthy beast. Oh well, he consoled myself, he had a good job for a Midgaan. Serving as the night watchman for the American was not bad work even though it had its difficulties. Most of the foreigners he had met spoke terrible Somali; his mistress was a little better than most, but it was still unpleasant to hear the sweet words of his native tongue so badly spoken. His mistress often said, "Osman, where were you last night?" and Osman thought she might be angry, but he just couldn't tell with these people. She sometimes said, "Osman, how can you guard my house when you are always asleep?" but she was smiling. He supposed she was teasing him, but it was hard to know what she meant.

Osman didn't really mind the quiet nights guarding the house on the outskirts of town. Hadija had been much kinder to him now that he had a regular job. He was careful to keep from touching unclean things, except for that cat who always wanted to rub on his leg. However, he took a lot of risks working for this American. Many in his clan said he shamed himself by associating with the foreign devils, but what is a Midgaan supposed to do? Osman didn't have flocks of camels or cattle to make him rich. He had only one lowly old milk goat. He had no money for a shop in the town. He lived as he could, by his wits and his cunning, and he was rather proud of that. Osman had a wife and five children, though most of them were grown. His face bore the deep furrows of raising them, finding enough food, money for clothing, and tea. His parents were dead, most of his clansmen were as poor as he, and they were scattered throughout Northern Somalia.

Osman was nicknamed *Osman Tuuk*, Osman the Thief. However, he was an honorable man to his own people. He took care of Hadija and his family, and honored his tribal relations. He only took things from people who did not need them. Could he be responsible if these foolish Americans paid large amounts of money for old camel bells and water jugs with holes in them? They wanted battered, faded, milk baskets that had already been used, ostrich eggs and porcupine quills. Why? Osman could hardly understand it himself, but he was a clever man and he could make a living by his wits. Osman might not be able to understand it, but that did not mean he did not profit by providing the things the foreign people wanted.

These Americans had lots of money and so Osman would get them whatever they requested. Well, there were many camel bells hanging on camels in the interior. Sometimes a foolish boy would be sleeping and the bell would just slide off the camel's neck, like so, and the lucky foreigner would have a wooden camel bell. Would these silly nomads sell you a bell, or even little woven mat? No, they would tell you to go and make it yourself. The women's work song goes,

> O weaving reeds, may you never
>   be poverty stricken
> May you never be taken for sale in the market
> May none be ignorant of your maker
> May no unworthy man ever tread on you.

If the foreigners wanted a camel bell there was no choice but to steal it. There was no other way to get these things. Osman would never steal a camel, that could have very serious consequences, especially for a Midgaan, but he would steal the bells. The nomads would never part willingly with their milk baskets, or prayer mats, they did not understand about foreigners, so Osman stole what he could. Most Somalis would not touch the bells again even if they found out where they were. The things had been in the hands of non-believers and were considered unclean by pious Muslims. No, the nomads would just make another milk basket or bell for their she-camel. They had nothing but time, and besides, they were richer than Osman, he reasoned, with all those camels. Osman would make a little extra money and the foreigners were happy.

Osman stole from the Somalis, not the Midgaans. Midgaans are not considered noble Somalis. The Somali tribesmen claim direct lineage to the prophet Mohammed. They claim that the first Somali people had floated on their sacred prayer mats across the Gulf of Aden from Mecca to Somalia. The Midgaan tribes remain outside the acceptable culture of the Somali people. Osman's kinsmen had found many ways to make a living, but not with the things anyone who considered himself a noble Somali would do. They would not guard the American's houses. Osman's kinsmen were the shoe makers and the butchers, jobs considered unclean by those who called themselves noble.

The next morning Osman's mistress gave him five shillings for saving the she-cat's life. The cat watched him from her perch on the back of a chair where she was busy licking her genitals. Osman's hand hesitated to take the money from the hand of the person who held the animal licking its genitals. However, he overcame his disgust and took it. Osman felt that he deserved a little *quat*. He hurried to the market to buy himself a little green bundle of chewing pleasure for the afternoon.

"Where are you going in such a hurry?" asked his kinsman, Ahmed. He was a cobbler in the lower market. He had a round face, rounded sparkling eyes, and a very round belly from all the money he made with his shoe business.

"To the *quat* market for some succulent leaves to chew this afternoon." Osman lingered to tell his friend about the scorpion and the cat, how he came to have a little extra money for himself. "I want some tender new leaves to chew. Has any *quat* come in from Ethiopia?"

"I haven't seen the trucks yet this morning," said Ahmed. "I did hear and see plenty last night, however," he continued. His eyes turned into little slits as he paused to smile at Osman's discomfort. Osman thought Ahmed must have overheard his wife shouting at him. Hadija had called Osman the son of a dog and she had refused to make his dinner because she wanted a new slip, she claimed hers was old and ragged. Osman had threatened to beat her and she had laughed at him. What is a poor old man to do, Osman thought. These women always wanted something or other. Allah knows he had no money to buy her a new slip, his back was bent with age and trouble.

"Will you chew alone?" Ahmed asked, changing the subject and catching Osman off guard.

Osman was caught. He could not refuse to share his little bundle with his kinsman. Later, if he needed something, Ahmed would not share. It was better to divide what you have, to keep good ties between clan members. Who wanted to chew alone anyway? "Would you join me?" Osman asked.

"Yes, Osman, what a good idea," Ahmed smiled and rubbed his hands together. They were smooth from working with the leather he used to make sandals. "I have some new poetry you might like to hear. My brother-law is visiting from the interior. If I brought him, we would have a fine *quat* party. You bring the *quat*." Ahmed's voice dropped with that little demand and he pursed his lips in expectation.

Now there would be three people to chew, and Osman only had five shillings. Why did everyone assume he was rich because he worked for the Americans, he wondered. He had five children and several relatives living with him. Osman had only one old goat to milk. Now he had to find a way to buy *quat* for three with money for one. He hoped there would be some old *quat* left over from the day before, or some bigger and tougher leaves they would agree to sell him for a cheaper price. Osman suspected this would take some hard bargaining. Everyone thought he had lots of money because he worked for the American. Osman knew it would be hard to get a good price, hard to get enough *quat*. Oh these foreign infidels, they brought so much trouble to the county, he thought. He wondered if saving that cat was bad luck and he should have let the scorpion bite her. It always brought trouble to interfere with the will of Allah.

After his trip to the *quat* market, Osman hurried up to the little circle of huts where he lived to tell his wife that she should prepare for a *quat* party. Osman, her husband, would be chewing that very afternoon. She should hurry and sweep for his guests and arrange to borrow some pillows from the neighbors, and a radio, so he would have a nice party. Osman would be the honored host, he thought, as he climbed the hills outside of town.

His wife, Hadija, was milking the goat when Osman came over the hill to their little compound. She placed the goat's head between her legs in the endless folds of her skirts. This kept the goat still since it could not see or move while it was being milked. She bent down over the back of the animal to reach the udder. Hadija grunted at Osman from her bent position. Her temperament was as unpredictable as the *goo* rains. Sometimes she blessed him with freely given little teases, sometimes she tormented him and withheld just what he needed to keep from suffering. She finished milking and placed her hands on her hips. She handed the milk *dhill* to their daughter, and stood unmoving. She was a big woman, with broad hips and long arms. The goats knew better than to struggle when Hadija did the milking. She was a solid rock, this Hadija, only her dress was softly fluttering in the wind. Osman's wife was not a flutterer. Osman began to wish he had not planned for this *quat* party. He kept the two bundles hidden inside his *goa* so she would not see them just yet. He began to speak but she interrupted him.

"Where is the tea?" she said and her words hovered in the air, like a scorpion looking for a place to strike the person who dared to disturb it.

Osman had forgotten to get some tea. He stood there holding the *quat* tightly against his thin body, wondering how he could possibly explain these green quat leaves, but no brown tea leaves.

"Osman, I asked you to bring us some tea. We have none, and I haven't had any all week." She paused, then invoked moral injustice, "What kind of a man will not provide a little tea for his family?"

"Sweetheart," Osman began boldly. "Never mind about the tea. I have wonderful news." Hadija stared at the bulge in his goa.

"It better not be news about a *quat* party," she replied spitting the words at him like bullets. The scorpion had found its target and was ready to strike.

Her tone made him tremble, oh, she could be fearsome this wife. The Quran accords women the right to be protected rather than to be independent, but obviously Hadija had never read the Quran. Although she could not sit in council with the elders of the clan, the elders knew they had better not cross her.

"I am talking this very afternoon with our kinsman, Ahmed, about a position in his shoe shop for our son." Osman sounded a lot more confident than he felt. The words hung in the air for a moment. The scorpion's spirit had made him toy with fate and he waited to be crushed.

Hadija's eyes lit up, and Osman was hopeful. They needed something for their lazy eldest son to do. Ibrahim liked to go about the town causing trouble with his equally indolent friends. Perhaps Osman could convince Ahmed to teach him the shoemaker's craft while they chewed quat that afternoon. Then he could set up a little stall in the market and sell shoes. A little frown began to creep over Hadija's solid jaw, so he added "Everyone needs shoes."

"You talk with Ahmed everyday," she said suspiciously. "Why have you only now decided that he should teach our son? Ahmed has sons of his own."

"We will discuss the arrangements this very afternoon," Osman lied, praying to Allah to forgive him. Hadija was doubtful, but for some reason she decided not to question Osman any further. Osman suspected she was willing to accept this story because she was so eager for even a slim chance for her son. "Hurry and prepare the house," he told her. He waved his little bundle so she could see it, "I have some *quat* to soften his resolve." To Osman's immense surprise and relief, she actually turned into the *aqual* and began shouting at the children to sweep the floor.

All that afternoon, when Osman should have been enjoying the *quat*, he was thinking how he would bring up the subject of his idle son to Ahmed, who complained on and on about how hard his shoe business was and how the people tried to cheat the poor Midgaans.

"You can't make any money with shoes," he lamented.

"I pay for the leather and the stall in the market. I have hardly anything left to feed my poor family. How lucky you are to work for the American. You have nothing to do but take home your money."

"I was thinking my oldest son might like to learn the art of shoemaking . . . ," Osman began.

"What?" Ahmed answered, rolling his eyes up to heaven. "Osman, why, oh why, would anyone want to condemn a young man to a life of hardship and insults in the market. Nobody is buying our fine leather sandals. People are all wearing those rubber thongs imported from China. They're cheap and don't protect you from thorns or scorpions, but people buy them all the same. It's really hurting business these days." Osman could see that there was no way he was going to talk Ahmed into teaching his son.

It was late when Ahmed and his rapacious brother-in-law left. Osman hurried from the hut in darkness to his mistress' house. "Osman," he heard Hadija's voice calling, the words tumbled over the hillside after him. It was not the tone of a lamb calling for help. Osman pretended he did not hear her and picked his way carefully over the rocky path that followed the edge of the town to the American's house. The American and Osman were both outcasts of Somali society and had houses on the outskirts of town. Osman lived in an *aqual* built by his wife of woven mats placed over bent poles. The American lived in a stone house with several rooms and a cement courtyard in the middle, but she was an outcast, like Osman, all the same.

Jeanne was waiting for him with a reproachful look. "You are late again, Osman. The moon has set, it's dark," she said.

What do these Americans understand about time, Osman thought to himself. How could he have gotten there any sooner? He had hurried. She had not been robbed. What reason did she have to be so upset?

"Osman," she continued, "I am having some people stay with me for a while. I will need to use the back room. I want you to start guarding the house from the outside."

This had been a longstanding issue between them. She

wanted her night watchman to sit up all night outside her door. Osman felt that it was too cold for his old bones, he was the night watchman so she should give up this idea. There could be wild animals or spirits roaming about the town, waiting for an old Midgaan with stiff limbs to prey upon. She just could not understand that Osman was not a young man any longer. He really did not want to be out all night in the cold: his bones ached, his back hurt in the morning.

This complaining had started last month when a thief had reached in between the bars on her bedroom window with a stick. The robber tried to draw objects from the dresser toward himself with the stick. He had picked up the radio that stood next to the bed and had awakened Osman's mistress when it crashed to the floor. She had rushed outside the house and chased the *tuuk* away with her screaming.

Unfortunately, Osman had not awakened. He had been sound asleep in his little bed. It was a chilly night and he was wrapped up in his *goa*. He was an old man and needed his rest. Osman did not hear his mistress until she came running into the back room and interrupted a dream he was having about saving the village from a screaming witch who had flown into their midst on a silver bird. The mistress had been very angry and had threatened to send him away. How could she do that, Osman wondered. He had worked for the Americans who lived in this house for many months. He came with the house. She was not moving. He and his family and clan depended on this money. How could she even consider sending him away? What would he do? How would he live? These Americans were really very strange to Osman. He worked for her, he couldn't just be sent away. Osman suggested she give him money for *quat* so he could stay awake at night. Osman thought it was a very good solution. She flew about the room with a red face and said things about no more money for a useless guard.

Now she would not change her mind. Osman would have to move outside the house. When he left his boss the next morning, he wandered into the town consumed with troubles. He had no bed and no tea. That squalid cat had a soft pillow and all the milk it wanted. Osman thought about a way to get some tea for Hadija. He wanted to go back home and be petted and sleep in the afternoon after a good meal.

Osman passed by Ahmed, in his stand in the Midgaan section of the *suuq*. Ahmed greeted him cautiously and Osman knew that something else was wrong.

Osman had a premonition that whatever Ahmed had to tell him was going to get him even more upset than he already was. Ahmed had an *aqual* in the same compound as his. Osman wondered what had occurred last night that his kinsman was so eager he should hear it and suffer.

"Oh the wailing, the crying kept us up all night," Ahmed said looking into Osman's face to watch his reaction. "None could sleep. Just have a look at my poor eyes, they are all red because of the dreadful noises that disturbed my dreaming. Your wife has the loudest, most piercing crying I have ever heard. All the women were with her. She was tearing her hair, throwing ashes from the fire, rolling on the ground outside and scaring the little children to death, until the women finally quieted her this morning.

Surely, Osman thought, Allah wanted to get rid of that cat who sleeps right on the soft bed of the infidel while Muslims are exposed to hyenas roaming in the night. He should have let it die, it was the will of God. Now he was punished with no bed, no tea, and a crazy wife. Osman hurried home with the tea Ahmed had given him. What would a man do without his clansmen? The compound was in turmoil when he entered. Cooking pots and bits of clothing were thrown all about, the fire had gone out, and ashes were scattered all over the place. It looked as though baboons had been playing there. Osman called for Hadija and women came screaming out of the *aqual* like a pack of wild dogs. There is nothing worse than women who are bent on your slow destruction. They will nip you to death.

"Osman, Osman, Hadija is very ill," they were all talking at once.

"She's been up all night moaning and crying."

"She tried to throw herself into the fire to stop the

pain."

"We had to hold her to keep her from wandering off into the desert."

Suddenly, as if to prove the point, sounds of wailing and moaning came out of the dark interior of the *aqual*. They paused, mesmerized by the increasing moans when suddenly Hadija appeared at the door.

Her hair was all astray and stood up around her head. She was a bulky woman and was frightening as she groped at Osman with staring dark eyes which were glassy and intense. She had bleeding gashes in her face and her dress was torn. She was screaming and reaching for her husband. Osman tried to comfort her and was locked into a frantic and painful embrace for his trouble. They both fell down in the scramble. When he finally extracted himself from her grasping hands she crawled after him and grabbed at his *ma'aweiss*.

"Hadija, sweetheart, what is it? What is wrong?" Osman asked, gasping for air. It was hopeless to talk to her because she lay writhing on the ground, kicking, biting at the dust, and shaking. She would not speak to him.

The women carried her back into the *aqual* and laid her on the sleeping mats. She moaned and screamed for what seemed like half the morning. Finally the sounds got softer and subsided, but she was a strong woman and could writhe for a long time. Mercifully the sweet peace of Allah's desert returned. Osman sat outside the hut and wrung his hands. He was exhausted from sitting up all night and he needed some nice tea and rest. He lamented that he had a curse on his life from a stupid scorpion.

"She is quiet now, Osman, you can come in," called her cousin.

Osman entered the *aqual* and sat down on a little three legged *michilis* next to his poor, suffering wife. He held her hand and she turned to him in her misery. Only moans came from her mouth and her head rocked back and forth as if he were really not there. Sometimes she talked to unseen people telling them to leave her alone and stop hurting her. She clutched at the air with her hands as if reaching for something but there was nothing there. Sometimes she would open her eyes and ask, "Allah help me, I am lost."

"*Habibe*, I am here," Osman responded. But no, she would say she was at her mother's house, or on a truck somewhere. The women made the tea he had brought and she sipped it weakly, never looking at Osman, only moaning in pain. No one brought Osman any tea and he was afraid to ask.

There was nothing for him to do. Osman left during the afternoon and gathered some old pieces of wood from his brother-in-law. He was sorry for Osman since his sister was acting so strangely and gave him some nice big boards. Osman carried them to his mistress' house to build a little shelter to protect himself from the wild hyenas. He built a box just outside her door that was big enough for him to crawl inside and sleep at night while he was guarding her house. The cat watched perched on the window sill.

When the American came home she said, crossly, "What is this, Osman?"

"It is a protection from the wild animals, " Osman told her. She shrugged and went inside to touch the infidel cat and then to eat her dinner with the very same hands.

When Osman went home the next morning, he was greeted by a deathly silence. His wretched wife was laying inside the *aqual* and had not moved all night. She was weak and feverish. The women were concerned. She had not eaten anything and would only sip a little tea from time to time. Osman skulked about the place like an unwanted relative, feeling as though somehow he had caused this, and that he had better do something to make this better. No matter what happens, why is it always the husband's fault, Osman wondered. The poor man wandered around the compound for a while but could not endure the reproachful looks from the women who had taken over the place.

Osman gathered some bits of tin and went back to the American's house. He used the tin to make a better roof for his shelter and to reinforce the sides here and there with patches held against the sides with big rocks.

His mistress was angry about the growing guard house.

"Osman," she snarled, "How can you guard the house if you are sound asleep inside this thing?"

Osman explained about the hyenas in the town these days and the damp air getting into his aged bones but she did not understand, or maybe she did not want to.

Osman's poor wife was ill all week. She languished all day in the *aqual* and she would hardly eat anything. Her sister decided to call the medicine woman to see why she did not get better.

The old woman was blind in one eye and the shriveled socket gave her a fearsome look. She stared at Osman with the good eye before she entered the *aqual*. He could hear low moaning and talking but he could not follow the words. The medicine woman came out and stood over him as he sat squatting in the courtyard, squinting with that grotesque eye. "Hadija is being tormented by a *saar*," she said spitting the words at Osman. A *saar* is an evil spirit that frequently takes possession of women who are despondent. "Your loyal wife has become so unhappy she has no strength to fight off this spirit. She does not care anymore," the medicine woman continued, reproach spilling out of her mouth like an overfilled milk vessel.

"What can I do?"

"You must make your wife want to live again, so she will banish the *saar* from her body."

"How can I do that?" Osman whined, hoping for pity.

"A new petticoat would help. Hers is old and torn. She has nothing soft and beautiful next to her skin."

"A new petticoat?" Osman had no money to get his beloved a new petticoat. There was no place to turn but to his mistress, his benefactor, his rich employer. Surely she would understand her obligation to help his family, he thought. His wife was ill, surely she would help him cure his wife of this affliction.

"Jeanne, I must talk to you, Hadija is very ill."

"Osman, I am so sorry to hear that. What can I do to help?"

"I need money."

"Osman I know the doctors at the hospital in Hargeisa

and I know they will help. Of course I will pay the hospital bill."

"She doesn't need a doctor, she needs a new slip."

"A slip?"

"She has become possessed by a terrible *saar* spirit."

"Hadija is possessed?"

"Oh yes, mistress. It has been terrible this past week with her moaning and crying. I can't get any sleep. This spirit won't leave her body. Some presents would make her fight off this dreadful *saar* and force it to leave her alone."

"Osman, I am going to give you some important advice."

"*Hiiyea*." Osman knew he was in trouble when she said that.

"Your wife is manipulating you. You must not give in to this, or she will learn it is effective and do it again. Osman, just ignore this and you can teach her a lesson. There is no such thing as a *saar*."

Osman could not convince her that Hadija had been possessed by a *saar*. This American woman just would not believe him. He guessed they do not have such spirits in America so Americans do not believe in them. That was a good protection for her, but Osman's wife did believe in spirits and that is just how one got into her. Now that she was possessed, she was not going to believe that there were no spirits. Osman was not foolish enough to go to his wife and tell her the *saar* was all in her mind and if she just ignored it, it would go away.

Osman gave up pleading with the American and went outside to add the final touches to his guard house. He added more tin patches to the roof to keep out the rain and put a few extra rocks in case of wind. He put an old straw mat for the floor to keep him warm. He had just crawled in and was enjoying his little bed when his mistress came out of her house and stood outside the door.

"Osman," she had a way of saying his name, this woman. "Osman," she said, like a teacher to a naughty schoolboy. "You are just going to crawl into this hut and go to sleep. You are supposed to be my night watchman. How can you watch anything from in there?"

Osman could see her feet just fine and they gave him an idea. "Mistress," he said crawling out of the box. "I think you need some new sandals. Your shoes are worn and old. I know someone who has some lovely new leather and will make you an exquisite new pair."

"Really," she said looking at her feet in surprise. "Well I guess these are getting a little old." Osman thought she regretted being so hard on him about the *saar*. Then she asked suspiciously, "How much are you charging me for them?"

"For you, mistress, only twenty shillings."

"Osman, I know that the price for a pair of shoes is ten shillings, and I am not paying double because I am American. If you want to sell me some shoes, ten shillings is all I am paying."

"Fifteen."

"Ten"

"Twelve"

"Okay twelve, and that is all I am paying."

The American went inside to get some paper and a pencil for Osman to trace the outline of her feet. He traced both carefully and rolled up the paper. He would take it to Ahmed in the morning.

Ahmed agreed that an evil spirit had gotten inside Osman's wife and was causing her illness. "She didn't look right on the day of the *quat* party," he said. "She just wasn't as sharp as usual."

"I don't know what to do about Hadija," Osman confessed. "I need to buy her a new petticoat and I don't have much money. Give me a special price on these shoes for my mistress," he pleaded.

"If you are charging her twenty shillings, I will make them for fifteen."

"Ahmed, she has lived here for a while and she speaks enough Somali to know that shoes are ten shillings."

"That is the price for a Somali, not for an American."

"I know, but these Americans don't understand that things are priced differently depending on who you are,"

Osman sighed loudly. "I could not convince her to pay more than ten shillings." (Osman silently asked that Allah forgive him for lying to his kinsman.)

"Osman, that's totally ridiculous," said Ahmed. He had a hard time understanding foreigners and how they thought. He fingered his worry beads for a long time, clicking them against each other as he considered the situation. "Osman, you and I, we live by our wits."

"Hiiyea."

"If we lose our cunning we will not survive in this world, Allah be praised."

"Allah be praised."

Then, Osman's dear friend Ahmed told him how to sell the shoes for twenty shillings, and, he said, the American woman would be grateful.

Later than week, when Ahmed had finished, Osman went to see his mistress. "Look," he exclaimed, "look at the beautiful leather and the workmanship. This is an exquisite shoe, it will protect you from stones and scorpions."

"Osman, I like the shoe very much," she said trying it on. It fit perfectly. "But, Osman," she continued, as he had known she would, "where is the other shoe?"

"Other shoe?" Osman said slowly innocently staring at the ground.

"Osman, I have two feet," she said holding up two fingers and waving them in his face. "What good will it do me to have only one shoe?" She looked exasperated.

Osman wrung his hands and put them to his face, "Oh, sweet mistress," he lamented, " you said you would only pay twelve shillings. That will only buy enough leather for one shoe. Things have gone up in price these days, because of the drought you know."

"Osman, how could you do this to me, you thief!"

He could see that she was angry, but there were little wrinkles in the corners of her eyes that betrayed her. "Oh, beloved mistress," he purred. "I decided that one beautiful shoe would be better than nothing. After all, what could I do for you with only twelve shillings?"

"Osman Tuuk, you deserve your nickname better than

anyone I ever met," she said. "Here! Take the other eight shillings and get me my other shoe."

"Oh, mistress," he carefully continued the lament, "each shoe costs twelve shillings these days. What can I get for eight shillings that will match this beautiful shoe."

"I can't believe I am doing this, I can't believe you are doing this to me," she said violently rummaging around in her bag and handing the twelve shillings to Osman.

Osman hurried into town to buy a goat to roast, spices and rice to stuff it with, and yards and yards of white cloth for his dear Hadija to make a new slip. The religious *mullah* agreed to come to the feast and recite holy passages of the Quran to drive away these evil spirits.

"Ahmed, I need the other shoe," Osman said, his arms full of gifts for his wife as he embraced his kinsman warmly. A man needs his clan in times of plenty and in times of trouble.

Praise Allah! The holy prayers, the special dancing, and the gifts worked a miracle. Osman's wife Hadija recovered her strength and fought the troublesome *saar* out of her body. She was soon up and shouting orders to everyone around the *aqual*. His dear wife kept the tea hot and the scorpions away.

Blind
Kindness

*Teaching is reminding others
That they know just as well
as you.*

—Richard Bach, *Illusions*

"Is it big or little?"
"Both."
"Is it bigger than this tea shop?"
"Sometimes."
"Is it smaller than bee fart?"
"Sometimes."
"Does it move?"
"Yes."
"Can it move as fast as a gazelle?"
"Hiiyea."
"Is it alive?"
"No."
"What color is it?"
"It doesn't have a color."
Well I was stumped, much to the delight
of my companions. We were sitting out-
side the tea shop in the shade of the
ancient banyan tree for my daily Somali
language lesson.

The teachers at the school, and the villagers in Arabsiyo, took great delight in teaching me a new word every day. They were pleased about my growing ability to speak Somali. They bragged about my proficiency and allotted me prowess in the language far beyond my actual ability. Somali is one of the most difficult languages for native speakers of English to learn. Only two dialects of Chinese are more difficult, and I struggled with every sound and phrase. The word for the day was *"dubayshay."*

"Is it a truck?" I asked, getting exasperated in direct proportion to their gloating.

"No."

"Do people make it move?"

"No, it moves by itself."

"I give up," I said, piqued by the ever increasing delight my companions were taking in confusing me. "What can be bigger than a tea shop, moves faster than a gazelle, but is not alive?"

Subti was pleased to have won the game. He leaned back in his chair to savor the moment. His clear brown eyes sparkled as he blew into my face and held my hand up to feel the breeze. *"Dubayshay,"* he said.

"Of course, the wind!" I didn't think I would forget that word. "I never would have thought of that," I said, shaking my head at the obvious answer. "You are clever teachers." The five handsome men sitting around the table that afternoon smiled, nodded with satisfaction, and slapped each other on the back. This teaching the American to speak was not an easy assignment, but they were used to the challenges of life in Somalia and rose to this one with gusto. Oral traditions are prized above all else in a bedouin culture. They are the tangle of threads that bind people together. Language is the only way knowledge and behavior can be passed from one generation to another. People say, "I have to hear it to believe it." Not being able to speak was a hardship my friends found intolerable for me. They were determined that I should learn to speak Somali so I could pass the days in easy conversation and hopefully learn proper ways for a woman to behave.

Subti was one of the teachers at my school. He was nicknamed Subti because of his hot temper. *Subti* is the Somali word for Saturday, the day after the Muslim holy day, Friday. Many people are short tempered when they have to go back to work on Saturday, therefore Subti's nickname. Subti spoke excellent English and was a godsend to me. Often he was the only person who could explain what was going on in a way I could understand. Abdul Kader was another fellow teacher. He was about the same height and age as Subti, but more filled out. He struggled with English and always listened carefully to conversations I had with Subti. Abdul Kader was a somber person with great hopes for a scholarship to study abroad. He had been waiting to hear about his application to a school in Germany ever since I met him, but no word ever came.

Ibrahim had no business that I ever knew about. He liked to sit in the tea shop and I didn't trust him, I don't know why. He was always polite to me, but I felt he was waiting for an opening, to catch me at something. He had deep-set eyes and a long chin. He was restless and couldn't seem to sit still. He drummed long fingers on the table, tapped his foot or stroked his forearm. Omar and Hassan were townspeople who had been sitting at another table and had joined our little group out of curiosity. They wanted to see if what they had heard about the white foreigner was true or not.

The tea shop was a ragged sort of affair even though it was the nicest of the three in town. It had sprawled out in the shade of the big tree and was supposed to be painted blue. Inside it was smokey and hot due to the central charcoal cooking fire. There were low wooden tables and seats dug out from the mud walls. The interior had been whitewashed at one time, but the monsoon rains and baking sun had caused the walls to crumble bit by bit. The floor was packed earth and quite soggy since it was a catch-all for left over tea, dirty water, and spilled food. It did get swept every morning, but in the afternoon it was necessary to watch where you stepped, except that it was hard to see in the dim interior. Human sweat, animal remains, spice tea, roasting meat, rice, and of course, *ghee* filled the place with odors you could see when the light was low and slanted in the late afternoon. There was a battered tin roof that leaked when it rained, which wasn't often. There were no windows, only a large wooden door to drag across the front of the place and close it at night. Although it was the best restaurant in town, I doubted it would ever be listed in the Michelin guide to Somalia (if one were ever written).

No one sat inside during the day, leaving the cook to shout at Ahmed, the kitchen boy, in peace. Outside, the rickety metal tables were held together with rusty wire and bits of string. The chairs were equally dilapidated and I always chose mine with care, and sat slowly, holding on to the table. Despite the shabby furnishings the tea was sweet, the conversation was lively whether I could understand it or not, and the afternoons wore pleasantly onward.

Abdul Kader fiddled with his radio to change it from Radio Hargeisa and purely Somali songs and poetry, to Radio Ethiopia which broadcast American rock during the afternoon. When he finally located the station amid the static of the Third World, the strains of "I Wanna Hold Your Hand" drifted over the scene. The Western music was quite out of place, like a warm day in the middle of winter. It reminds you of a different time of year and makes you uncomfortable. It's nice but it doesn't fit, and you know it won't last.

Somali songs are complex and filled with luminous imagery. They are the culmination of the oral tradition:

All your young beauty is to me
like a place where the new grass sways,
After the blessing of the rain,
When the sun unveils its light.

When I translated lyrics like, "I wanna hold you hand" into Somali, no one would believe me. My companions were convinced that I just did not know enough of the language, they couldn't accept that "I wanna hold your hand" was the most complex idea expressed in this famous American song.

That afternoon the conversation drifted into a heated

argument about my nickname. The two major contenders were *"Dehab,"* or gold, and *"Chino,"* or fermented camels' milk. I did not want to be called "Chino" since I had strong feelings about being described as milk that has been buried in the desert for two weeks and used to intoxicate the nomads. However, I could see that I was not going to have much to say about this, as usual. Nicknames are given out according to what others observe about a person's nature and the stories that are told about you. You don't get to choose one that flatters your vanity, you get told something about yourself. Subti accepted his and acknowledged his temper, but it was hard for me to accept that people thought I was wild, crazy, and smelled bad.

Since I lost the word game, I signed a chit to pay for everyone's tea. A cup of tea cost two gumbos, so I was out a shilling-two altogether. Not enough to break my budget. I had more money from my $100 a month Peace Corps salary than I could ever spend on the few items available in the little village.

It was the first of the month and that night, Ali Yare, Ali the Little, would come to my house. He was a village elder and the owner of one of the general stores in town. His daughter-in-law, Amina, lived in the house next to mine. Probably because of her insistence, Ali Yare had adopted me as sort of a poor relation. He had named me to the Saad Musa so I would have the protection of a tribe and had even offered one camel toward my bride price. The villagers didn't think that would help me land a husband, however. They often discussed my slender chances of marriage right in front of me, as though I were a child. I supposed that it was indicative of how they felt about unmarried women. Too thin, too ugly, and can't make good *"ghee"* was the consensus about me. *Subughee* was a rancid sort of butter churned in milk baskets, or *dhills*, from camels' milk. I hated it, it smelled nasty and tasted worse (to me). I never could eat it and it was liberally poured over everything edible in cold globs. However, one did not insult mothers' special *ghee*, and I never said a disparaging thing publicly about this delicacy of the desert. I did request that I be spared having it on the food I ate, however. Everyone assumed that was why I was so thin, and encouraged me to eat a little *ghee* to fatten myself up while I was young and still had a chance to catch a husband.

That night, a little after sunset, I drank my evening meal of warm milk mixed with a little sugar because it tasted of the charcoal used to clean the milk baskets. I filled my lamps with oil and lit them with one of my precious matches. I had heard that the match factory in Mogadishu was on strike. Near the equator, there is no lingering twilight that gradually wraps the earth in shadow. When the sun disappears over the end of the purple horizon, it is pitch black almost immediately, like a door has been firmly closed.

I was just coming out of the long drop, when there was a polite knock on the rickety wooden door of my house. I forgot to take my lamp with me when I went to answer it, still expecting light switches. Abdillahi, my headmaster had borrowed the flashlights I brought back from Hargeisa and never returned them, so I peered out into the darkness. I knew better than to expect it was my night watchman, Osman Tuuk. He didn't show up half the time and even when he was there he quickly fell sound asleep in the back room.

Ali Yare was quietly standing there with his nephew, Ali Abdi, one of my students. They did not notice the forgotten lamp. They were used to walking in darkness and accepted the night instead of trying to change it. Ali Yare was short as his nickname implied, about five foot seven, and he had a round face and belly. He was, however, immensely dignified rather than jolly. Ali Abdi, at perhaps thirteen, was already taller than Ali Yare. He had the same round face and the perfectly designed Arabic features of his uncle. Somali boys were often raised by their father's brother and Ali Abdi lived in town with his uncle so that he could attend the new school. Ali Yare had been instrumental in seeing that a school had been built for the village children. The townspeople had provided the labor, U.S. Aid had supplied most of the materials.

Ali Yare carried a cloth sack filled with little pieces of

paper. These were my chits. The elders had decided it would be better for me to sign a chit when I wanted to buy something after they observed that I had no idea how to handle money. On my second day in the village I had presented one of the ragged beggar children with an entire shilling. He had looked at it, and back at me in surprise, not knowing what to do any more than I understood why he did not just take it and run off. By this time, four other equally tattered children appeared and pleaded for money. Their bare arms were so thin you could see the radius and ulna outlined through the tight smooth skin. They all had eyes too large for the protruding cheekbones in their faces. It was the extruded teeth and ears, that seemed two sizes too large for the head, that shocked me. I stood there in the street, unsure of what to do. Subti saw this impasse from the tea shop, and came over to help me. He explained that the gift to a beggar is a gumbo, or two at most, if the giver is wealthy. A shilling, or ten gumbos, was just too much, the beggars expected the appropriate gift. "Go get change and everyone gets two gumbos," he said to the boy holding the shilling. All the children ran off to the tea shop for change, smiling and grateful, now that the offering was proper. Subti explained that if a beggar boy had a shilling, people would think he had stolen it. I promised to do better in the future. When I thought about it, a cup of tea also cost two gumbos. At home in the States, a cup of coffee cost a quarter, and that was the expected gift to street people. However, in my country, a beggar would instantly run off with a ten-dollar bill from a stupid foreigner. Here, life was ordered by the will of Allah and people struggled to accept the vicissitudes of their existence, not to change it.

Even though I had lived in Arabsiyo for several months, I still hadn't the slightest idea what people meant when they told me what things cost. I could barely count to five: *koe, laba, siddah, afra, shun*. I got totally confused when a merchant said that oranges were two for three gumbos and six for five unless I wanted the little ones that were fifteen for a shilling. As a remedy, the elders had devised the chit system for me. The merchant, or tea shop waiter, wrote down the cost of my purchase on a piece of paper so I could understand what I was paying, then I signed it. I was grateful for Arabic numbers. I rather enjoyed this Somali Mastercard, until, of course, the end of the month, when Ali Yare came to present me with the final bill.

I did most of my shopping at Ali Yare's shop, so Ali saved the little scraps of paper in a battered cloth sack. I would usually use a chit to pay my bill at the tea shop, and other shops in town. The owner would then go and collect cash from Ali. At the end of the month, all of the chits were gathered and Ali Yare came to my house with Ali Abdi, for what I called the "chit ceremony."

Ali Yare would slowly take the chits out from the sack one by one. He carefully read off the amount to Ali Abdi who would write it down. He passed the tattered little scrap of paper to me for my approval. After we had looked over all of the chits, Ali Abdi would labor over the addition. He would add the long column of neatly printed numbers two times and come up with the same answer. I was grateful that Ali Abdi always came up with the same final number. I worried that I would not get the same number twice and politely declined to check his work.

When Ali Abdi had calculated the final total, I would count out the money into Ali Yare's hand. It was always a small amount, not nearly the 1,000 shillings I was paid each month. There was little that I wanted to buy in Arabsiyo, at least not that I could discover. What could you buy in this untroubled town with three tea shops, and five general stores which all carried the same things? There was a small open marketplace or "suuq," where the farmers sold lemons and oranges from the orchards when they were ripe. Occasionally someone slaughtered a goat, and put the meat up for sale, but how much can one person eat? There was nothing to buy beyond the very basic things which sustain life. Money and material possessions were not the measure of a person in Arabsiyo.

Ali Yare and I would wait quietly in the little circle of the lamp's soft light. In the darkness outside my door, cattle walked by on the way back to the compounds where they spent the night. Ali Yare sat imperturbably, fingering his prayer beads lovingly, at peace with himself and his place in the world he knew. I fidgeted on the wooden chair, leaned on the table, crossed and uncrossed my arms and wondered how I could stop my thoughts from constantly flying about my mind like a torrent picking up everything in its path. Sitting quietly with a guest, and doing nothing, was nearly impossible for me. I was used to filling up little corners of time with small talk, but I didn't speak enough Somali to make such conversation. Ali Yare and I sat together and I listened intently to the little sounds a pencil makes on paper.

After the total was agreed upon, I told Ali he was lucky to have such a clever nephew. Ali Yare told me that Ali Abdi was lucky to have a teacher and go to school. I was making small talk, Ali Yare was not.

After Ali Yare and Ali Abdi left, I began to prepare the lessons for my classes the following day. I taught English, social studies, science, math, gym, and art. Each class had about fifty students, sitting on twenty-five battered chairs at five elderly metal tables, a few pieces of chalk, and no books. I spent my evenings typing out exercise papers or stories for my classes to read on the only typewriter for two hundred miles. I had a spirit mimeograph machine so I could make copies of lessons for my students. When I could not make copies, I had to write everything on the board. If my students didn't copy correctly, they learned mistakes instead of proper English. The lack of materials and equipment made teaching difficult, but my students were so eager to learn, and so smart, it made up for everything the building lacked.

The only book any of the boys or teachers had was *The Student's Companion*. This was the only educational publication I ever saw in Somalia. Ali Yare had a copy or two for sale in his store but I didn't recommend anyone buy it. This edifying epistle was written by Wilfred D. Best, the former Inspector of Schools in the British West Indies and was originally published in 1950. The book had a washed out orange cover, 237 pages, and not a single illustration. It was written expressly for schools in the British colonies and I guessed it was supposed to be a one-book school.

Northern Somalia was a British protectorate for seventy-five years from 1884 until 1960 and the educational system was based on the English model. The Somalis said that the British left no bastards, meaning that they lived apart, and did not mingle with the natives, or understand them. *The Student's Companion* was a good example of this. It was always a surprise to me how well some people spoke English given the confounding contents of that book.

I couldn't understand what Wilfred intended the book to teach. I think it was supposed to contain everything an educated person living in Africa needed to know, and I wondered what Wilfred knew about Africa. It was a book of lists and the most useless tool for teaching that I could imagine. It was divided into eleven sections: Single Words for Phrases and Sentences; Figurative Expressions; Proverbs; Big Words for Small Ones; Geographical Facts; Abbreviations; General Knowledge and Civics. It was a compendium of totally useless information. I sometimes wondered if my intense dislike for the book could be due to some defensiveness on my part. Much of the vocabulary was new to me despite my college degree from a fine university. I believed that words I did not use as a native speaker were not very important for non-native students to master.

The book began with four pages of lists of words denoting numbers. I thought of using some of them in letters home to impress my grandmother, but never had a sentence that would fit the words.

A number of leopards	leap
A number of peacocks	muster
A number of cats	clowder
A number of savages	horde
A number of hired applauders	claque

I was afraid that if I wrote home about a clowder of cats, Grandma would think I was making some kind of Somali soup. This scintillating chapter continued with:

Names by Which Persons with Certain
Characteristics are Known:

One who is opposed to intellectual progress	obscurant
One who eats all kinds of food	pantophagist
A noisy, abusive, scolding woman	termagant

Well, having eaten camel and goat meat, I suppose I was a pantophagist. However, I have a rule about not using words you can't say and I was afraid of what perversion people would attribute to a pantophagist.

The book went on to more gripping topics such as:

DEATH

Murder of a brother	fratricide
Murder of a sister	sororicide
Murder of a parent	patricide
Murder of a king	regicide

There were no less than ten pages of proverbs. The Somalis have many wonderful proverbs which reinforce appropriate thought and behavior. They are powerful teachers in an oral culture, but I could only imagine what my students made of Wilfred's selection:

A man's house is his castle.
Christmas comes but once a year.
Call a spade a spade.
It is folly to live in Rome and strive with the Pope.
The Queen can do no wrong.

The Somali word for vagina is "seal" and the book had a story about the Queen and her royal seal. My boys had no end of fun joking about the Queen putting her royal seal on all official government documents. Who could say anything if the Queen can do no wrong?

The book was a veritable treasure trove of trivia. For example, I didn't know that the shallowest sea in the world is the Baltic. Most of my students had never seen a sea and hadn't any notion of shallow.

There was a section on similes in case students wanted to write an essay or give a speech. I hoped that my class would not use phrases such as:

> as joyful as a fly
> as lawful as eating
> as smooth as ice
> as unattractive as a gargoyle

I explained that a gargoyle is an ugly beast placed on the outside of buildings to keep evil spirits away. I was not surprised that my students had absolutely no trouble understanding that concept.

In his preface to the section on small words for big ones, Wilfred admits that he put the section in the book "simply to provide mental recreation, and to help those who take part in quiz contests."

BIG WORD	SMALL WORD
pellucid	clear
nigrescent	blackish
acataleptic	complete
labefaction	defer
contumelious	insolent

The educational purpose behind much of the book was not at all pellucid to me, but I decided not to be acataleptically contumelious about it. I just did not use it in class and so I was forced to develop my own materials.

Because Somali was not a written language, all the international and written commerce had to be conducted in English. I knew that my students would most probably man the infrastructure of the bureaucracy responsible for running the county in the twentieth century. They would be the bank clerks, the airline booking agents, the tax collectors, and the governmental administrative officers. I was determined to give them a practical, useful education in English. I wanted to provide lessons which reflected their lives, within the context of a country struggling with modern technology.

I had brought a visa application back to Arabsiyo from my last visit to the American Consulate in Hargeisa. I copied the form for a visa to the United States on my typewriter to reproduce for my classes. I had decided that being

able to fill out a form in proper English would be useful to
many of my students, and a few of the teachers. I wanted
my class to understand what information was being requested and why. I thought it would be a good skill for my bud-
ding bureaucrats. I made enough copies of the form for both
of my English classes, standard six and standard seven. I finished preparing this special lesson just before the gas in the
Tilly lantern ran out and the light sputtered and coughed
itself to death. Well, I mused, "A man's home is his castle,"
and went to bed as joyful as a fly.

The next morning I was eager to begin my new
improved English lessons. After the boys had finished scraping the naked legs of their metal chairs across the cement
floor, I handed out the visa application form and we started to go over it together.

"Put your name on the top line, last name first," I
began.

"Which name?" asked Ali Abdi, waving his hand in
front of my face.

"Ali, your first name is Ali and your family name is
Abdi, so you write Abdi first and Ali here."

"That's just my name from my father. Where should I
put my name from my father's family?" he asked, serious-
ly concerned. "What about my grandfather's name, and the
name my mother gave me?"

That was a very important question, and I had not
even considered it. These forms were not developed for
people who are given names by both the father and mother and whose main identity comes from their tribal lineage.
The tribal lineage goes back for generations and is lovingly
taught to little children as soon as they can talk. It is proudly recited for Grandpa when he comes to visit, like an
address or telephone number in the states. It is, in fact, the
nomadic address. Socio-economic class, occupation, world-
ly possessions, and significant others can all be determined
by the tribal lineage. It was not going to fit on this little line.
Determined not to give in, I made a snap decision.

"Girls put the name given by the mother, boys the
name given by the father," I said, hoping I would remem-

ber this bit of logic for my next class. "Your father's name can be the middle name and your grandfather's name the last name." My students were confused, but I hurried on to the next line hoping to avoid any further consternation. However, it was not any easier.

Name turned out to be the easiest bit of information requested on the forms. Date of Birth was more perplexing. No one knew the exact day, month, and year of their birth. The students had been born at the time of the flood, during the new moon at Ramadan, or when the locusts had swarmed and eaten the grain.

"Okay," I said to quell the commotion that erupted over date of birth, "You are about thirteen years old so you were born in 1955. Let's count off from one to twenty-eight. Everybody in the first row was born in the first month, the second row is the second month, third, fourth, fifth and sixth. Take your row number and put it on the month line, your count-off number for the day, and we'll assume the year was 1955." We only had six rows of chairs and that is why none of the children in Arabsiyo were born from July to December in 1955, and no one was born on the 29th, 30th, or 31st. It was the best I could do.

Street address posed still another problem. Half of the children came from the *aqual* camps outside of town and did not want to put Arabsiyo on the address line, like the town boys. Desert dwellers felt morally superior to the boys who lived in town. However, desert was hardly acceptable as an address, neither was interior. I finally came up with, "Arabsiyo, environs of." We never did get to the end of the form and it was the last time I tried such a lesson. It was just too difficult to translate nomadic ways of organizing the world into the lines on a Western form. My parting words were, "Be sure and sign the same name at the bottom as you put at the top." Then I shook my head in disbelief over what I heard myself say.

This foray into the twentieth century had ended like most others, in turmoil and trouble. Many of the boys were upset about the absence of a place on the form for the tribal lineage. This is the most important piece of identification for a Somali, not an address which changes with the rains and the grasses. The boys were beginning to suspect that the Western world did not understand their ways and they found it rather insulting. They didn't appreciate me for pointing it out either.

I took the long way back into the village after school that day. I wanted to think about why my lessons always seemed to end up in chaos. The desert was even and calming, it had a special stillness which settles over the centuries on places where life never changes. I decided I just had to learn more of the language before I could hope to be a more effective teacher.

Near the dry river bed where the greenest grass grows, I stopped to watch a little boy. He was about six or seven and had been sent out to watch his family's flock of goats and see that they did not stray off. His hair was soft looking and nubby and incredibly long silky eyelashes encircled his large brown eyes. I knew he could speak this difficult language at six better than I ever would, no matter how hard I tried. He was pleased at seeing me, a distraction from the long afternoon with only the clouds and locusts for company. He came to stand near me, but not too near. I wanted to make a nice comment about his goats but I couldn't recall the word for goat.

"What do you call these animals?" I asked.

"Ah," he said beaming at my interest, his total face involved in his smile. "This is Asha, that's Faardumo, over there is Dehab." As he called them, the little goats scampered over for a pat and looked me over with curiosity. It looked like a scene right out of *Heidi* except for the lack of Alps. I wondered if I would ever get any of my questions answered.

That afternoon I stopped at Ali Yare's store to buy a bottle of spirits of alcohol. I used the spirits for my duplicating machine and had used what I had for the visa application. The store was a one-room conglomeration of people, children, sacks of rice and grain, scarves, drums of gasoline, tea kettles, three bolts of cloth, all the same (from which every single dress in town was made), tins of pineapple and mango juice, sugar and tea wrapped in cones of paper. People bought what they needed to make one pot of tea, they did not store up a week's supply. The shop was the centerpiece of gossip and news and most people visited every day. There were other things tucked up in the boxes and cartons that were piled precariously behind the counter. I couldn't buy them because I didn't know what they were called in Somali, and I had not been able to explain that I wanted to look at things, just to see them, not to buy them. Everybody knew everything that was in the stores already, except me. Subti said he didn't think there was a word in Somali for curious. Nobody was curious, because they already knew everything. I couldn't explain to Ali Yare that I just wanted to browse among the assorted goods, so I was limited to buying what I knew I needed. I was sure that Madison Avenue would be quite dismayed by that novel nomadic idea, only buying what you needed. I had brought my bottle of spirits to show Ali Yare that it was empty. I turned it upside down in front of him and shook the empty bottle in case he did not understand what I needed. Ali Yare said no, he was out of spirits. I went on to two other shops but they were out of spirits as well.

There seemed to be a distinct lack of spirits in town lately. It was expensive and most people only used it to start their Tilly lanterns. These are made in Great Britain and are similar to Coleman lanterns in the States. I knew how to use them from my camping days. In fact, living in Arabsiyo was a lot like camping. There were no kitchen counters to wipe or toilets to flush, very wild countryside, an occasional wild animal, and lots of mosquitoes at night. You pump the base of the lantern to get some pressure. In order to keep the gas flowing up to the flame, you need to prime the lantern with spirits of alcohol and light it to draw the gas in the base up to the top. The spirits of pure denatured alcohol burn off quickly and are replaced with the slower burning gas. The Tilly lamps were used in the tea shops and stores when they stayed open for a few hours after dark. Most people did not use them, they were noisy and gave a rather harsh light. I used mine to correct school papers and read a book before I went to bed. Usually, the gas would run out just as I got to an exciting part of the book. I would read faster and faster as the lamp sputtered for a while and finally coughed itself out. It seemed to always leave me in darkness at the most exciting part of the book. I often went to bed in the dark wondering whether or not Bilbo would escape without putting on the ring or something.

A Tilly lamp needed only about a teaspoon of spirits to get it to light. Most of the spirits I purchased were poured into my mimeograph machine to make school papers for my classes. I had brought a supply of paper back to the school from Hargeisa during my last visit. I just went to the Commissioner of Education and asked for some paper. He had been very surprised at my intrusion but had opened a very spare closet and given me some. I had mistakenly thought that I was learning how to get things done. Now I didn't have any fluid to put in the mimeograph.

I did not go to the tea shop that afternoon. I had army ants parading all over my house. I had squashed them, and tried to divert them, and had gone all the way around my house killing everything in sight, but they just kept marching. I had removed all the food, set out bowls of water and dug trenches, no success. They seemed impervious to my every effort. They traveled all around the outside of my house in a line and then into the door in relentless, maddening single file. I asked Amina to come and look at them.

"Hiiyea," she said, agreeing that I had ants.

"Amina, I don't like the ants," I told her searching for the sentences I knew in Somali.

"Hiiyea," she replied.

"They are dirty."

"Hiiyea."

"I don't want them."

"Hiiyea"

"Will the ants go away?"

"Enshallah, If Allah wills," she replied.

I tried another tack. I led her all around my house again, pointing to the line of ants that never stopped parading. Then I led her around her own house and looked for ants. Then I said, "Your ants are dead."

"Ah," she replied, finally understanding what I wanted. "*Deedeetee'ga.*" So after all that, D.D.T. was called D.D.T. in Somali. Western products came too quickly to be assimilated into the language. There was no word in Somali for many new things, and a syllable like *'ga* was tacked on to make the English fit in with the natural cadence of Somali. Laundry soap was called *tide'kee*, petrol, *petrol'dee*, and truck was *truck'grayaa*. Assia, my friend in Hargeisa, told me that speaking Somali was easy. "Just add *grayaa* to every *phrase-grayaa*" she said, "and that is Somali."

The next day I went over to Ali Yare's shop to buy some *Deedeetee'ga*. While I was there, I asked again if he had gotten any more spirits.

"No," he said, "the truck has not delivered any."

I had some papers I wanted to duplicate for my classes so I urged him to hurry and get some more for me. "Please order at least five bottles for me," I told him. I decided I would stock up and avoid running out again. "I really need it," I said, hoping he would hasten to find another source for me. Ali Yare only looked at me sadly and I smiled to reassure him. "I am really grateful for all your efforts to get this for me," I said.

I took my folded paper packet of D.D.T. and sprinkled it around the perimeter of my little stone house. The band of ants that had marched relentlessly around my humble abode for weeks disappeared in a single afternoon. Better living through chemistry, I mused, secretly so glad that I didn't have ants, that I didn't care if D.D.T. caused thin-shelled bird eggs.

That night I went next door to visit with Amina, her mother, Howa, Nurah, her house girl, and little Cosa. Howa sold frankincense and myrrh in the market. She was a thousand years old, with the smiles of well-kept secrets in her eyes. She had been divorced by her husband because he wanted to take a third and younger wife. She had come to live with Amina bringing Cosa, the daughter of her husband's second wife. The wives had felt that life in the desert was too difficult for a little girl and that she should go to Quranic school in Arabsiyo. Cosa was a sparkling child of about seven who laughed at the day and had a sweetness only possessed by unspoiled little girls.

I liked to watch her play with the other children. The girls made tents out of their father's *goas* and the boys sneaked up and scared them. They all played tag and a game similar to hopscotch with lines drawn in the dirt. How do they know these games, I wondered. I considered the possibility of a primordial knowledge of play genetically coded and needing only a friend to inspire its release.

We were sitting on a mat around a little brazier of coals left from the day, when Ali Abdi came looking for me. "Ali Yare wants to see you," he said. I wondered what Ali Yare could possibly want. "He is coming to your house with the other headmen." He explained this to Amina in Somali and she looked over at me with her eyes open wide in surprise.

"Spirit-kee," she said and I agreed. A spirit must be whispering bad things about me to the elders. I could not imagine what I had done to result in a visit to my house of the village elders and hurried to make sure my living room was clean. A woman's primordial response to trouble.

"I'll make tea," said Amina, tucking stray wisps of hair into her scarf, another primordial response to trouble.

I lit my Tilly lamp and both of the little oil lamps. Then I sat and listened to their hissing, hoping for an answer to what was going on. A knock on my wooden door and Ali Yare appeared, his composed face a comfort to my questions. He and seven of the village elders entered my house.

They had brought Ali Abdi, perhaps as a translator, and as was customary in this village, Hassan N'Asse the mad man shuffled in behind. It would have started a scene had I asked him not to come in. He picked up the mood of the group and squatted in the back of the room mumbling slowly and carefully to himself. He had a way of being present for all village councils so it was official if Hassan N'Asse was there. He had sense that evaded most of us and probably knew more about what concerned the elders than I did.

The men quietly arranged themselves around my little living room sitting on the four chairs, and the little stools or *michilis* that Cosa brought. "Would you like some tea?" I asked.

"*Hiiyea,*" was the polite reply.

I was anxious about what the trouble was and fretted as we waited for the tea. I could not imagine what I had done to offend the elders. For the most part I had tried to live quietly and stay within accepted bounds of appropriate behavior. True the children always managed to dig up my garbage no matter how I tried to hide it. I waited until late at night to take it to the village dump and buried it away from the main garbage pile to escape detection. However, last week I had discovered Cosa and her little girlfriends playing with little dolls they had fashioned from my tampax tubes.

I had decided to accede to the request that I wear long skirts to teach in the school, especially the adult night school, so I would not cause the men to become aroused. The Somalis do not find the breasts especially sexy, but revealing a leg is considered quite provocative. I wore my head covered as the Muslim women did, so as not to insult the religious leaders, and I stayed away from the mosque so as not to sully it with a female presence. I wondered if they were going to tell me to stay away from the tea shops. Women never went to the tea shops. That must be what is upsetting everyone, I decided.

Amina brought the tea and we served the hot sweet liquid to the elders. I did not open a package of crackers knowing that they would be suspicious of any food not prepared in the village since I was known to be a pork eater.

Ali Yare cleared his throat and the room became quiet. He spoke slowly in Somali looking at me and pausing so Ali Abdi could translate. "We are pleased that you have come to teach in our new school," he began. "We built it as a village because we want our children to be educated. We know that you are far away from your family, and that you are often sad. We can see it in your face."

"*Hiiyea,*" I responded in agreement, touched that they observed me so closely.

"You have taken a Somali name, Chino, which pleases us."

"Hiiyea," I hated being referred to as sour camels' milk but I would not argue with Ali Yare.

"We know that you are not a Muslim and are free to drink alcohol."

I was surprised. Although Abdillahi, my headmaster, had repeatedly asked me to bring him some gin, I had not brought any to Arabsiyo. I knew that the elders would be highly offended and I feared what would happen if I started to supply Abdillahi. It was illegal for him to buy it, but I could as an infidel.

"If you continue to drink, it will make you blind," he said gravely, looking at me like a father concerned about a child.

"Tell Ali Yare that I am not bringing alcohol into the town." I said to Ali Abdi, afraid that I would say the wrong thing if I tried in Somali.

"He says the elders know that you are drinking too much alcohol," was the reply.

"I am not drinking any alcohol."

"The elders say that you should not deny this, they have only come to warn you that you will go blind."

I sat there bewildered and the silence of our mutual confusion settled over the group like a fog.

"Ali Abdi, tell them I don't have any liquor."

"Teacher, they say you have bought up every single bottle of spirits of alcohol in town. Today you asked Ali to get you five more bottles."

I began to laugh with relief and Hassan the Fool, joined my laughter from the back corner of the room. The others stared at this strange American laughing for no reason, like a hyena.

"Please come to the school tomorrow and I will show you what I am doing with the spirits. I use it to make ink on the papers for the boys, I don't drink it. You are right, these spirits will make you blind if you drink it, but I am not drinking it."

Ali Yare was satisfied and nodded his assent. He rose

to leave. The others followed his gesture, and the little group moved with great dignity out of the house and into the quiet streets. I knew they would talk far into the night about this new information. The alcohol makes ink for the school. They had seen the papers I gave to the students and were eager to see how this blue writing came from the spirits which were clear.

Abdillahi paid me a visit after the elders had left. He wanted to know what they had to say to me. When I told him what had transpired, he laughed contemptuously. "These elders don't know anything," he snorted. "They are just a bunch of ignorant men from the desert."

Abdillahi expressed the conflict brewing in Somalia between those who had power from the traditions of the long honored past and those who had authority brought by involvement with the modern ideas arriving so quickly in the country. Who could win this struggle? Could it be resolved peacefully or would violence erupt? I feared it would end in a bloody war like our own Civil War. The modern (North) against the traditional (South).

Well, I thought, unwilling to contradict my headmaster, the elders know about people, and they observe the faces of those in the village. They know that I am often lonely and frightened. They humor Hassan the Fool, and they are concerned for all those who live here. In the course of living a life, this is probably more useful information than how to fill out a form. The simplest questions are the most difficult to answer. Who are your parents? Where are you from? Over a lifetime these answers change.

The
Promise

A woman is like a shadow: go to her, she flees; leave her, she follows you.

—Somali Proverb

One warm afternoon my friend Asha came to visit me from Hargeisa bringing her friend Assia. I had attended Assia's wedding on my very first night in Arabsiyo. I had been frightened by the loud singing and shouting and returned home. When Assia told me the story of her wedding I was overwhelmed by how much I didn't understand about Somalia, and how much I missed in every event I attended.

Even by Somali standards, Assia was a beautiful young woman. She had perfectly spaced features, light skin and long eyelashes framing overly large brown eyes. She was clever and curious about everything, especially Americans, and we became good friends.

She had been offered in marriage by her father to a man she did not know. He was much older than she. On her wedding night her infibulation was cut open in order to allow for intercourse and that was why the women had been shouting. I had been alarmed by the excitement and left without understanding what was going on. Oddly enough, Assia told me, she and her husband, Hajji, fell in love. She found the American way of finding husbands very intriguing and told me every detail of her own marriage.

Assia's Marriage

The afternoon when I first heard of my father's intentions for me was hot and quiet, even the goats were still. I did not nap that afternoon because I wanted to clean my teeth. I put a piece of charcoal into a little wooden bowl and pounded it until it was a very fine powder. I rubbed this onto my teeth with my finger. Then I used the soft stick from the corday tree as a toothbrush to scrub the charcoal up around my gums and on my teeth. This keeps your gums pink and healthy and your teeth bright and shining. I did not want to be a toothless old woman. "There are only two kinds of women," my father's second wife told me, "beautiful women, and those who do not know how to make themselves beautiful." I intended to be beautiful.

The children were sleeping on mats inside my cousin Delmar's house. I had come to visit and help her with a new baby, her third son. My closest friend was Delmar's sister, my cousin Faadumo. I wanted to spend a little time in the interior away from my home in the village of Arabsiyo. In the bush outside of the towns and villages, the air is sweet and soft, the nights are starry and filled with laughter and stories told by the firelight. My cousin's mother-in-law was a fine storyteller. She kept us up late into the night with tales of Aroweillo, the eccentric Somali queen of the Habr Toljaala. *Habr* means "mother of" and when it is prefixed to a name, it signifies all the descendants in the female lineage.

"Aroweillo," mother-in-law began, "kept everyone in the entire clan under her tight control. She hated men, did not want any interference, and succeeded in having all the men castrated. Her daughter however, was at least as clever as her mother. She found a way to keep her own son from the queen and he helped the Habr Toljaala to outsmart Aroweillo.

"Once it was very dry and the camels needed water. Each morning the people would go to Aroweillo for permission to take the camels to the wells. 'Not now,' she sighed day after day in a high squeaky voice, 'I am too busy.' Then she would turn her back and say, 'I have to wash my little finger.' "

"Weeks went by like this and the Habr Toljaala were desperate. Finally Aroweillo gave in, but she demanded that the people bring her branches from the thorny acacia that grow near the river. 'Each camel must carry back a load of the thorn tree's branches,' she ordered. The people knew the thorns would pierce the camel's skin and wound them severely on the long trek back to the grasslands. They went to Aroweillo's grandson who was kept hidden in a milk basket to ask his advice.

"He knew how to outsmart the cruel queen. 'Make the camels sit on the banks of the river,' he told them. 'Cover their backs and sides with a thick layer of river mud, then put the acacia branches on top of this. It will protect them from the sharp thorns.' The people did as they were told. Aroweillo was furious and knew that they had a secret advisor, but she never found him."

My musing about the Habr Toljaala was interrupted by the sound of running feet. Why would anyone run in this heat I wondered? "Assia, Assia! Where are you?" my cousin, Faadumo came into the courtyard calling my name and running like a scared goat. She was very skinny, this cousin. She had long legs with knobby knees like an ostrich. Her movements were always brisk and her reactions impulsive, but I loved her because she was quick to laugh as well.

I waved at her to be quiet and pointed to where the babies and the new mother were sleeping. I couldn't talk because of the charcoal in my mouth and I showed her my black teeth, parting my lips like the camels when they are angry.

"Assia, Assia!" she exclaimed, ignoring my gesture. "Your father wants to see you! He sent for you," she danced around me, her gentle black eyes flashing and smiling, her long dress whirling.

"Suq," I said, wait, between rigid teeth. I didn't want to swallow any charcoal, get it caught in my throat and choke.

Faadumo, that lively goat, would not stop. She tilted her head slightly up, put her tongue forward and began to ululate, the high-pitched warble used to signal great emotion. I threw my toothbrush at her in disgust.

It caught in the folds of her swirling dress and she picked it up and began to kiss it passionately as if it were a lover. She danced around the room and I could hear the baby begin to whimper. I picked up the cup of water I had prepared to rinse my mouth and threatened to throw it at her, but water is too precious to waste. I only shook it at her, then rinsed my mouth and spit in her direction.

Faadumo sat on the mat beside me. She was talking like an entire flock of birds in the bushes. I rinsed more of the charcoal dust out of my mouth, and spat it out on the ground. "Faadumo," I said dryly, *"wallaahi, wa dusa mareb* (you are the fart that never ends)." It was a little joke between us because Faadumo had been born in the village of Dusa Mareb. Even this did not stem her flurry of words from blowing about the courtyard and into my mind, like a wind with nothing to do but cause trouble.

"Ibrahim came on the truck this afternoon. He has come to take you to your mother. Your father says you must come to him right away."

I had not seen my father for several months. He, two of my brothers, and other members of our family, had taken our camel herds into the interior. They wanted to fatten up some of the stock and ship it to Saudi Arabia where there was a market for camel meat. Ibrahim was my father's brother, from my grandfather's third wife, and he was about my same age. If he had come to bring me home, it must be important.

I spit some more water from my mouth into the dirt at the side of the woven reed mat. It made a little wet spot, but was quickly absorbed because the ground was so dry. "Get the baby you little goat," I said to Faadumo. I wanted to think about this. My mind was racing like a frightened gazelle with danger at every turn. Of course it must be about a marriage. But my girl friends were choosing their own husbands these days. I hadn't met anyone I wanted to marry. Who could this stranger be? " Oh Assia!" chattered Faadumo, blinking as she came out of the black interior of the house with the baby. The sun after darkness makes your eyes hurt, like finding out a lie. "A wedding, you are going to have a wedding. Your father is negotiating your bride price, your mother and his relatives have agreed. *Hiyii*" Her excited yammering made the baby cry.

I was getting angry with Faadumo for having me married off with nothing to say about it. I snatched the baby from her and sat him on my lap facing me, supporting him on my bent legs. I cleaned his runny nose with my fingers, and flung the slime into the dust. My heart was pounding and I held the baby next to me to quiet myself as much as him. I positioned him between my open legs to see if he would make water.

If Ibrahim had been sent to bring me home, it must be important. Ibrahim was *mud medow*, a very black-skinned man, and had a nasty side to his personality. I did not like him. Once he started a fight in the market and struck a woman in an argument about the cost of a goat. Her clan claimed she had lost her unborn child. Injustice to a woman is considered a moral injury to the men of her tribe and the *quadi* had set the compensation, or *muk nagod*, for the injury to the woman and the death of the child, at five camels. Ibrahim disputed the decision and refused to give any of his camels in payment. My father tied him to a tree and threatened to kill his livestock, one after the other, right in front of his eyes if he would not pay his portion of the compensation. He started with Ibrahim's favorite she-camel. He held the knife at her throat until Ibrahim relented and paid the woman's clan. We were all glad that he did not have a gun because he probably would have killed someone. For days afterwards he stormed around like a wounded elephant. The elders were furious at Ibrahim and his hot temper. They sent him away from Arabsiyo and made him live in the interior for several years, tending the camels. My father agreed that it would be good to calm him down and keep him out of trouble.

Faadumo had me married off with three sons and as many goats by the time Ibrahim arrived. When he strode into the compound, his long shadow reached all the way across it and ended at my legs. He told me that tribal relations had approached my mother about a marriage. Usually marriage proposals are first discussed by the female members of the two families. If a man sees a woman he would like to marry, he will discuss it with his mother. She will visit with the female relations of the girl and decide if the match would be suitable. If the women agree, further discussions will take place. My mother and my father had decided it was time I was married. Ibrahim said that my father concurred with my mother and they had settled on a husband for me.

"He is a rich man, Assia," said Ibrahim quietly, without looking at me. "You are a lucky girl." I did not nod or ask him to continue, but stared at my hands folded in my lap. They were sweating as if I had been pounding grain all afternoon. "He has a big fine house in Hargeisa, you will have everything you want," Ibrahim said. I thought of the proverb: "The wife of the rich man lacked a ring." Nobody has everything in life, I did not love this man, I did not want to marry him. I was angry with being told about this decision by someone I disliked. Angry that I had not been consulted.

That night, lying on the sleeping mats inside the little house with my cousins and the babies, I couldn't stop angry tears from running down my cheeks and into the corners of my mouth. I didn't feel lucky. I was frightened. Who was this man? Would he beat me? Hargeisa? I didn't have any close relatives in Hargeisa. Slowly, carefully, I felt my body between my legs, the tiny opening, big enough for urine and blood, not big enough for a man's penis to enter. I remembered the searing, throbbing pain of my infibulation when I was closed. What about my promise? When I was little, this idea of promising to sleep with a man, despite the pain of being opened on your wedding night, was a joke, a game. We all sang the songs and bragged about it. Now that all seemed so stupid, I couldn't believe I ever joked about it. I hated this man and I never wanted him to touch me. I didn't want to be cut open so this stranger could enter my body.

Years ago when I was about as tall as the late grasses, during the year of the many rainy days, my mother had taken me to the Midgaan woman. She had infibulated me and all of the other girls in the village who were my age. I remember that it hurt very much for a long time. It had been so painful to make water, I had cried every time. My legs were bound together by long strips of cloth and I used a stick to hop around the house. I was soon tired of that game, but my mother kept the wrappings on so that my vagina would heal tightly closed, like a proper woman. My mother and grandmother brought me sweet things to eat and many presents including a gold bracelet. When I cried, my mother would shush me and tell me about how brave adult women are and that they never cry in pain, never whine and never complain. "They are strong and elegant no matter what, *ebb, ebb-way* (shame, for shame)," she responded sharply to my whimpering. She did this to make me tenacious and admirable and I believed her when I was as tall as the grasses.

My mother and grandmother told me that on her wedding night a woman is cut open so that her husband can penetrate her. All of her new female relatives, and her own kinswomen, will witness the cutting, to affirm that she is still a virgin. This honors the family. Then they return in the morning, after the groom has left the wedding bed, to see if the bride is still bleeding. If she has fulfilled her promise to sleep with her new husband, despite the pain of her opening, then they will dance through the village and announce to everyone that this is a very strong woman to be respected and revered. It had sounded exciting to the grass girl, now I was afraid and afraid to show my fear.

My mother was an unyielding woman. I had never seen her cry, never seen her discouraged at anything. She had high cheekbones and her eyes sat right on top of them and saw everything. Her beauty came from her elegant and graceful walk, the dignified way she sat and carefully gathered her long dress about her. She was never ruffled, never out of control of herself or those about her. She had flocks of sheep and goats which she had nurtured over the years. They had grown from her *ma'her* or the portion of the bride price which goes directly to the bride as her own. My mother had tended her herds carefully and was now a wealthy woman. She had a special relationship with my brothers who helped her with the animals. They took her side in any dispute, and represented her interests in tribal decisions. My father respected her and sought her counsel. Although he had younger wives, my mother ran the compound and kept everyone in line. "The first one makes the home." says the proverb. "The feet of the first wife do not walk in the dew of the morning," complained my father's second wife because she had to get up each day to make the early cooking fires. However, she didn't dare to complain in front of my mother. I rarely saw a tender side of my mother. I knew that I was not her first daughter. There had been another girl, but my mother never talked about what had happened to her. I always felt that somehow I was just not that lost daughter, that it was hard for my mother to love me. She left me in the care of my father's second wife most of the time when I was little. She had insisted that I go to Arabic school in Aden, she had defied my father about this and paid for it herself. Now she had decided on a husband for me. How could I defy her? Where would I go? What would I do? I did not want to marry this old man, this Hajji Mohammed Aden, even if he were rich and had no other wives.

Ibrahim had explained as much as he knew under Faadumo's persistent questioning. My mother had been approached by female members of Hajji's clan. They had come to assess my character and suitability to be a member of their family. My mother, her sisters, and cousins had talked over this marriage for several days. They had decided it would be a suitable match, and had approached my father and the tribal elders to make arrangements. My father had come back to Arabsiyo, leaving the herds in the interior with members of our family.

I knew that a match between two clans is very important and, once made, not easily broken. Even a couple who hate each other have a hard time getting divorced because of their clans. A man can divorce his wife by saying "I divorce you" three times. He must say "I divorce you" to his wife, to the elders of his extended family, and then to the elders of her clan. Unless there are already mutually bad feelings between the two clans, the elders will mediate, counsel, and pressure a man to keep his lawful wife. This is in order to prevent difficulties from developing between the two clans. A divorce is an insult to the woman's clan and the woman will have no one to provide for her. Often the clans will arrange a second marriage in an attempt to keep the first intact. I knew if I were married off to this Hajji person, it would be for the rest of my life.

When I arrived home in Arabsiyo, my mother and father talked to me. "You are a lucky girl, Assia," said my father. He had a white beard colored with henna. His long neck rose triumphantly from broad shoulders which were only slightly stooping with age. As a girl I had been afraid of him, now I was wary because of the power he held over my life.

"Hajji Mohammed is wealthy and generous. He will be a good husband," he said, looking into the distance. A fly walked on his beard, I wondered if it was trapped like me. I sat on the floor cushions next to my mother who held my hands. Hers were decorated with henna in intricate designs. Mine were sweating. My father continued, carefully choosing his words. The fly flew out of the room towards the light and I wished I was a fly. "He had one wife who died without bearing him any children. He wishes to marry again and have many sons." My father held his prayer beads in his right hand as he spoke, absently fingering the smooth beads which never left his side. I wondered if he slept with them. "Hajji is a member of our tribe, Saad Musa. He comes from a good lineage and will be a good husband to you. Our relatives say that he is a kind man, gives alms, and follows the path of the faithful."

I stared at the floor in defiance. I felt like I had when my mother had taken my favorite he-goat, *Hydigi*, Star, to the market to sell. "Assia, it's time to sell this goat," my mother announced one day and that had been the end of it. I had nothing further to say in the matter. Everyone haggled over the price, nobody cared that I would miss Hydigi's softness, that he greeted me in the mornings with a nudge, that I had raised him from a baby and knew exactly where he liked to be petted and scratched under his chin.

"Assia, you would be very silly to disagree with this," said my mother, rearranging the veil which had fallen away from her face. "Your father and I truly want the best for you." Seeing that my eyes were filled with tears she added, "Assia, of course you don't love him now, but you will learn to love him. You'll see." To her that was the end of it, just like my goat.

I did consider running away. To where? Or dousing myself with gasoline and burning to death like Zahara, one of the village girls. I wanted to live my own life, to make my own decisions. I hated everyone, especially myself because I didn't have the courage to do anything. Eventually I decided to burn myself to death after the marriage, if this Hajje was horrible.

The first time I saw Hajji was when he came to discuss the bride price. My father and brothers lingered in the courtyard that morning waiting for the arrival of the visitors. It would be insulting not to be waiting at the door for an honored guest. When Hajji arrived with his relatives, they were greeted formally; *"Ah salaamu aleekum."*

"Aleekum wa salaam," answered our visitors. My father offered a bowl of water for washing. He poured a thin stream of water onto the clasped hands of each guest and presented them with a little towel. Everyone received a

drop of pale green toilet water to rub into their hands and face before they entered the cool interior room of our house. My mother had prepared a goat stuffed with rice and spices and roasted slowly in a bed of charcoal. I could tell that she was excited about this marriage because she slaughtered one of her favorite goats. Mats and cushions had been spread in the room and the men sat in a circle. My mother and I brought in a tray mounded with rice, the spicy goat meat piled in the middle. I could feel Hajji's eyes looking at me, burning into my back, but I kept mine lowered. If he thought I would betray the slightest interest by looking at him, he was mistaken. I kept my head down and attended to the business of arranging the meal on the mat in the center of the room.

The men ate from the tray, taking a portion of the rice in front of them gracefully with the fingers of the right hand. The left hand is considered unclean and is used only for personal hygiene. The men joked about the government, discussed the high price of *quat*, and offered each other especially nice morsels of the goat meat.

"Hajji eats more than anyone," observed my father with a smile. A guest who does not eat well, insults his host.

When the meal was finished, my mother and I came to take the tray back to the kitchen. The women and children would eat what remained of the rice and meat.

The washing ritual was repeated at the end of the meal. My father held the water pot and poured a thin stream so the guests could wash their hands. They slapped a drop of toilet water on their faces.

We brought hot spiced tea and oranges to the men and cleaned the room in preparation for the *quat* leaves they would chew together. More pillows and cushions were placed around the whitewashed walls. A radio was situated near my father's cushion so the men could listen to Radio Hargeisa and Somali music, poems, plays, and the news. I brought in the *quat* so my father could give each man a bundle about the diameter of a woman's wrist. They would pull the tender green leaves off the slender branches, one at a time, and slowly, tenderly, chew them. After the leaf is thoroughly chewed, it is tucked into the corner of the mouth. This continues leaf after leaf, until the side of the mouth is full of *quat* and bulges out like a woman's breast.

My brothers had been to the *quat* market at noon when the fresh leaves arrived from Ethiopia. It was illegal to bring *quat* into the country, but not illegal to sell it. The *quat* market on "Fucking Street" was thronged at noon each day with the men from the village. The trucks used to smuggle *quat* into the country were fast, and could outrun the border guards. When the trucks could not make it because of the muddy roads during the rainy season, there were many *quat* runners. These young men ran across the desert carrying the day's supply of fresh leaves to the willing buyers in the village.

My brothers had been careful to buy *quat* with very small leaves, not stalks that were old and big. Small, young leaves are the most potent and therefore the most expensive.

I disliked men who had nothing better to do with their lives than chew *quat* all afternoon. *Quat* is a mild narcotic, it quells hunger and is a moderate stimulant. After an afternoon of chewing, some men will be up late into the night, wandering in the town, drinking tea and of course, endlessly talking, talking about nothing. They are useless, these men, and I hated Hajji for being one of them.

"See," I hissed to my mother in the kitchen as we cleaned the dishes. "That man will spend his life chewing like a cow with green spit running down the corner of his mouth."

"Assia," snapped my mother, "all important business, including the bride price is traditionally discussed and settled at a *quat* party." She stood up with her hands on her hips, "This does not mean that Hajji does nothing but chew *quat*. Don't you think I asked about him very carefully?" My mother waited for my response but I didn't look up. If you like him so much why don't you marry him, I thought. I didn't dare say it. I cleaned the dishes in a silent rage while the man talked and chewed, listened to the radio, recited poems, joked, and spat green juice.

I took some cold ashes from the charcoal fire and scoured the inside of the pots used to cook the rice. When they were clean, I used water saved from the cooking to do the first rinse. Then I used clean water from the jug to do the final rinse. Our water came from a tank on the top of the roof. A pipe ran down from the tank to the inner courtyard of our house. In the middle of the courtyard was a drain, and the cement floor was slanted slightly toward the middle. I could wash the dishes near the pipe and the water would flow in a little stream toward the center of the courtyard and down the drain. My ears were burning as I washed the pots and the faint sound of the men's talk drifted into the still afternoon. I didn't think they would be laughing and joking if men were the ones who got cut open on their wedding night.

I sat with my mother doing beadwork on a little handle for a miniature spear as the shadows moved slowly across the courtyard as they had every day of my life. This day was different and it was comforting that the shadow did not waver in its path. It did not leave a track as evidence of the events which transpired. Like the sun which cannot be retrieved once it has set, the talk that day could not be undone. I considered what the Prophet Mohammed said about marriage as I worked. He said that when husbands and wives hold hands, their sins disappear through the touch of their fingers. After I kill my mother, I'll hold hands with Hajji, I mused.

All afternoon my father haggled the amount of the bride-price with Hajji and the members of his clan. I sewed rows of green, white, and yellow beads in smooth rows in the handle of the dagger. The price was finally set at fifty camels to be paid by Hajji's clan to mine. Twenty males and thirty females. "Whatever costs you dearly, you will care for," said my mother, her black eyes glinting with pride. I thought she looked like she did when she made a good bargain on one of her goats. Her chin jutted out and there was a wisp of a smile on her lips.

Some of the price would be paid directly to my family, some would be given to members of the clan. Insults, murders, injuries, and marriages are all resolved by paying compensation in camels. A price to redress the injury, or compensate the bride's family, is agreed upon by the elders. The murderer, or the betrothed, must pay the agreed-upon price. The bride price must be paid because the woman will be injured, I thought, cut open on her wedding night to bleed for her mother-in-law. I was angry, I resented being treated like a piece of property, but pride at the high price Hajji would have to pay drifted unbidden into my thoughts. The thought of it brought a wisp of a smile to the corners of my mouth.

My father also agreed on the *ma'her* or the amount of the bride price to be given directly to me. This would be mine and I could keep it even if we divorced. Hajji had agreed to give me one thousand shillings, four gold bracelets, and ten goats which my mother and sisters would keep for me.

"Don't be a fool Assia," said my mother. "This *ma'her* is generous. Your father has done well for you." She handed me a *helo* or love poem from Hajji. He had lingered near the kitchen looking for me, but I did not come out and so he gave it to my mother.

> Your body is to Age and Death betrothed,
> And some day all its richness they will share.
> Before your firm flesh goes to feed their lusts,
> Do not deny my right to love you.

I crumpled up the stupid poem and threw it into the fire. I had a right to refuse this marriage.

My mother saw the paper flaming as it burned and sat next to me. "Assia," she said, "this man is not that old and has no other wives. His first wife died without giving him any children."

"I don't love him." I argued with her.

"You will learn to love him. He is a kind man."

"He is not attractive to me."

"Assia," she answered, "there are many things involved in a marriage. Kindness and wealth are good foundations to build a love. Poverty and meanness will pierce your heart like sharp thorns and empty it. You won't care for love when you are hurting or hungry." I didn't answer her. What did she know about love?

Over the weeks that followed, my mother talked to me many times about her own life, something she had never done before. One day, when we were alone in the courtyard, she told me this story. "When I was first married to your father, he was not a rich man. He gave most of the camels he owned to my clan for my bride price." She talked slowly, carefully, as if the words had been buried deeply within her.

"Our first child was a girl, which displeased my mother-in-law. She and I did not get along, she was sour like old milk. When this baby was just learning to walk, I became pregnant again." Mother sighed and stared past me before she continued. "The rains did not come, and did not come. There was hardly any grass left and the distance between the grasses and the deep wells got further and further. We walked to our wells, but they were dry. Your father ordered us to walk quickly to the deep wells shared with the Galla. The journey takes seven days and we had to hurry because the animals needed water. I could barely keep up because my belly was so full with my new child. I couldn't carry that little girl, she was too big. She kept falling further and further behind. I would go back to her to encourage her to keep up with us, but her legs were too short. My mother-in-law beat me with her stick. She told me to leave that baby or we would all die. "Forget about her you fool," she said. "Keep the child within, perhaps it will be a boy."

And so one long terrible afternoon I left that little baby in the desert. I heard her calling after me in her velvety, sweet voice, *"Hooyo, Hooyo."* There was nothing for it but to abandon her. I didn't have any choice but to put one foot in front of the other over those endless brown hills. I tried to close up my ears but nothing kept that little baby voice out of my mind. There was not even any tears or time for me to cry. Why do we struggle so to go on living when it is so hard and full of pain I thought? But, I couldn't stop myself from living, and I couldn't save that little girl. The only thing I could do was to walk."

I looked at my mother and saw that tears were streaming from her eyes making glistening tracks down her face. They stopped in the corner of her mouth then dropped unheeded from her chin. It was the first time I ever saw my mother disheveled. Suddenly she exploded into sobs and her body shook and jerked like it was broken. She cried as if this story had been inside her for so long that it had to tear her body apart to find a way out. I was frightened, I had never even seen my mother cry. I put my arms around her and we rocked together.

"Assia," she continued after a long silence, heavy with sorrow, "marry a rich man, so you don't have to leave your children on the desert." We sat together and watched the light give itself up to the long arms of the darkness. I put down the little spear handle and let the beads spill out of my lap. I felt my anger at her recede with the daylight. The story was like rain after a drought, it soothed the anger and the grief, but not the dread.

Hajji Mohammed returned to Arabsiyo several weeks later for the betrothal ceremony. I glanced at him when he came into the room and my heart was pounding like the wings of a chicken about to be killed. He was not attractive to me. He had a stubborn face, with deep wrinkles under his eyes and at the edges of his mouth. His narrow face was framed by large ears and tufts of hair. He did not excite me.

We went to see the religious advisor or *Quadi* at the white stone mosque on the edge of town. The *Quadi* took one of Mohammed's hands and asked him if he would promise to look after my needs. Hajji said "Yes," but he looked at the *Quadi*, not at me, as if his covenant was with Allah and not with me. His promise is spiritual I thought, mine involves a very real knife.

The *Quadi* asked me if I consented to the marriage. He did not take my hand because I was impure. Slowly I said, "Yes," because there was nothing else I could say, nothing else I could do. I said it without looking up, keeping my veil wrapped closely about my face. My heart was wrapped up too, safe from this intruder.

The *Quadi* recited from the Quran:

And whatsoever good ye do, Allah knoweth it.
So make provision for yourselves:
For the best provision is to ward off evil.
Therefore keep your duty unto Me,
O men of understanding.

My mother's insistence rang in my ears as I followed Hajji back to my house, hating him, hating myself. After he left, I told her, "I consent to the marriage, but tell him he better not touch me."

"Tell him yourself, you have a tongue woman," was her reply. I was a promised woman and no longer her responsibility.

I prepared for my wedding. "Hajji sends you this poem," said my mother one afternoon, holding a letter. It was another popular Somali poem written in Arabic letters.

I long for you, as one
Whose dhow in summer winds
Is blown adrift and lost,
Longs for land, and finds,
Again the compass tells,
A gray and empty sea.

"What costs you dearly, you will dearly love." My mother's voice rang in my scattered dreams. I wept because there was no way for me to refuse my body to him.

"If a girl has appointed a day to her fiancé, that day she must open up her hips," chattered bony Faadumo, who had nothing to worry about.

The wedding would last several days and nights and our relatives would gather from all over for the feasting and celebration. My mother took me shopping for a wedding dress. "Let me get this white cloth for the dress," I said.

"Assia, you agreed to this," answered my mother and she almost slapped me. White is the color of death; the devil is white. She suggested red cloth with bright flowers from an Arab merchant and I agreed. Red is a color of fertility and happiness. My mother sold several goats and purchased yards of cotton to make new slips and bedclothes for me. I bought a new veil from the shop in town. My father's second and third wives worked to embroider cases for pillows and cushions. We bought oranges, lemons, rice, tea, and papaya for the feasting.

My cousin, Faadumo, made a wedding *dhill*. She carved a small wooden container about the size of a young camel's head into the oval shape of the tightly woven baskets or *dhills* used for milking camels. She filled it with spiced meat that had been dried in the sun so it would not spoil. She sewed cloth left over from my wedding dress to shroud the *dhill*. Then she made a puzzle by tying an intricate series of strings around the outside of the *dhill* She carefully wove the strings around and around the little basket. Only one knot would untie the strings and open the *dhill* divulging the sweet meat inside. All of the other knots were false and would lead the person astray.

"This Hajji has to find the secret way to your heart," said Faadumo, "and I made sure he will have to work hard for it. "A woman is like a corn cob: you have no teeth, you hardly eat," she quoted. She laughed, flashing her teeth and holding up the finished *dhill* with satisfaction. I wondered about Hajji's teeth, I hadn't really thought to look at them. I bet he never even cleaned them and tucked his corday toothbrush behind his ear when he wasn't chewing on it like the nomads.

During the evening of the first wedding night there was dancing around a fire built outside our house. I stayed inside with my relatives and mother. It would be unseemly for the bride to join in the fun outside. Hajji came and sat on the cushioned mat next to me. We did not speak. He was quiet, and I noticed that he was shy with my mother and the older women. I didn't say anything to him but sat patiently with my veil wrapped around my face waiting for him to leave. He was an intrusion into my familiar circle. I thought about the intrusion he wanted to make in my body. He smelled of toilet water, and it occurred to me that perhaps he was trying to attract me.

The next day, in the late afternoon, Hajji came with some of his friends and male relatives. Faadumo and our girlfriends greeted them. Faadumo had a big stick. "Let's see if you are clever enough to find the secret of this little wedding *dhill*," she said. "How quickly can you untie these skinny little threads? It shouldn't be difficult for clever boys like you," she taunted the men. She struck Ahmed, one of Hajji's friends on the shoulder as a signal that he was first. He had long smooth fingers and a scar on his arm from a camel's bite. He tried to untie the knots while we teased him. This friend was too slow, too much like the silly sleeping sheep. Faadumo hit him again with the stick and told him to go home to his mother, maybe she would feed him. She struck another friend and we taunted him to find the sweet meat inside the *dhill*.

The men teased us back, "If you haven't seen the bride, don't unroll the sleeping mat."

"A wife is like a blanket," we answered, "cover yourself, it irritates you; cast it aside, you feel the cold."

At last Subti found the knot to the correct string and he opened the *dhill*. He was a handsome man and I liked him but he was noted for a hot temper. We all shared the sweet tidbits inside and continued joking and laughing far into the night. I felt safe and comfortable in the sweet circle with Faadumo and my other relatives. Hajji sat across from me and said little, but he laughed nervously. I began to look at him boldly to try to catch his eye. I wondered why he did not look at me directly and would not meet my eye, but joked so easily with that silly Faadumo, the fart that never ends.

On the third night the women continued to mock the men and dance outside in the flickering light of the fire. They were answered insult by insult by the men. Firelight teases and taunts your eyes, your mind has to sustain the images you want to see. Firelight sustains nothing.

"Woman is the source of all evil; only our soul saves us from the harm she does." chanted the men.

"Regular work tires a woman, but totally wrecks a man," the women answered.

There was a sudden change in the intensity of the dancing, the women's singing was louder, the men were silent, they had no answer to a woman's promise. The

Midgaan had come! I shrank back into the corner. My knees turned into loose sand, my mouth was dry. I clung to my cousin Faadumo. She was as frightened as I, I could see her blood pulsing in the veins that stuck out in her thin wrists. My mother entered the room followed by my cousins, and other kinswomen. Hajji's relatives followed, his sisters and his father's second wife. His own mother had died many years ago. The Midgaan woman stood in the doorway, silently. She was framed by the fire behind her and looked like an avenging angel to me. She waited to be invited to enter. The ends of her mouth curved downward and the curve was repeated by her sloping shoulders. I saw the glint of a knife she held in her clasped hands. Her bare feet were gnarled and thick with deep cracks from the desert earth. They had never been cushioned by shoes. Outside village girls were singing loudly, the men had retreated. Several women began to ululate and the pulsing sound filled the room until I could not hear. Then they came to the corner and dragged me into the middle of the room. I was crying. "No, mother, not yet," I sobbed, grabbing at her skirts. She took my face and put her hands over my mouth, willing me not to cry out in front of my new in-laws. Do not shame me, she said with her eyes. Bring honor to me, daughter.

She turned me over on my back. I could see the expectant faces of my new relatives, standing silently, watching my tears. I felt like my little goat, Star, sold and held down for the ritual knife as if ritual killing was not murder. I hated the women who came to watch and resolved that they would not have a show. I can stand pain without screaming like a little baby, I told myself. I lay quietly rigid but I knew my mother felt my sweating palms and heard my quick shallow breathing as I fought for control.

The women drew my legs apart and lifted up my beautiful red wedding dress. I remember that the sweet smell of incense filled the air, and that I could not see because of the smoke and the stinging hot tears in my eyes. The Midgaan woman knelt between my legs. I could smell the leather of the amulets she wore for protection. I prayed that her knife would be sharp and would not tear my flesh. Let it be sharp, not old and dull I begged Allah. Quick as a *dikdik* turns, she placed one hand on my vagina and put the tip of the knife into the little opening left by my infibulation. The blade was cold against my sweating skin. She eased the blade up and out, opening the entrance to my vagina, through the scar tissue. The cutting was quick and it was several moments before my body registered the pulsing pain. It surprised me and I screamed, but only once. She poured an ointment of oil of myrrh on the bleeding flesh.

My mother and Faadumo hugged me, kissed me, "You are a woman strong and beautiful, You do not flinch at pain," they sang. It was over quickly. I could sit up. I could feel the white hot burning between my legs but, yes, I can bear this, I thought. I could feel the sharpness, feel the blood oozing down my inner thighs, but I could stand this. My mother brought me tea. Faadumo, wiped my face and hands with a cool cloth dipped in sweet smelling water. My friends were singing and clapping. "A strong Somali bride. She is graceful like the camel. She is strong when the thorns of life pierce her, she is unmoved like the earth. She is unmoved." I was proud, but mostly incredibly relieved. I had not shamed my tribe, my mother or sisters.

Too soon the women left. I could hear them outside singing and taunting the men. "You are not as strong as women. Who of you could be opened on your wedding night? Did you hear a cry of pain? NO! Women are strong."

I was alone. I sat on my knees, not willing to get up yet, I needed just one more minute to calm my racing heart. The door opened, and Hajji entered the room but I couldn't rise. I sat on the floor in shame that he would see me kneeling, trembling, unable to stop my quaking, trying to catch my breath. I couldn't stop my heart from beating wildly, my hands from shaking, or use my legs to rise.

Hajji knelt down next to me. I did not expect this. He gently placed his hands on my back and stroked me. He took my face in his hands. I saw that his lovely bronzed eyes were filled with tears of concern. *"Habibe, habibe,* sweetheart, sweetheart," he whispered softly. He placed his face, soft, his hands, soft, on my face and whispered again,

"Assia, Assia." He put his arms around me and his strong arms lifted me gently to my feet. He whispered again, so softly, "Assia, my little Assia."

He fumbled with his clothes as we sat together on the bed. I could feel his great anxiety and it made me bold.

"Why did you want to marry me?" I asked.

"After my wife died, my family pushed and pushed me to marry again, Assia," he said. "They found wives without even talking with me. I was angry that they just took over my life like that. I am not so young, I am away a lot, I was content to just be for a while. But, no, people were at me constantly, pressuring me about not having any children and such. Finally I gave in, just go find somebody" I told them. He looked at me then and smiled. "My step mother suggested you, and I guess I really didn't care at first. Then one day, Subti pointed you out to me, you were buying some cloth in the market with Faadumo. I followed you for quite a while. You never noticed me, an old man, did you?"

"No."

"I wanted the marriage then, Assia. I've been lonely, my house is quiet. I know that you don't care for me. I can only hope that someday you will. My hands get sweaty when I think about you."

I burst out laughing at that, I just couldn't help it. I understood this feeling of being pushed around by your family, and I know about sweating palms.

We lay on the bed next to each other. He asked, "Are you hurting, my lovely flower, my little Assia?"

" No, no, I am not hurting," I lied.

Hajji left without speaking in the hour before the sun blesses the land. His silent moving away after our night of touching hurt me as much as harsh words. So this is marriage I thought to myself. This pain between my legs was like a sharp thorn, a fiery pulse, but I realized I could bear this without crying out, without showing my pain to anyone, especially Hajji. I discovered that part of a woman she never shows to anyone, not her family, her friends, her husband, or her children. I thought of my mother and her inner accumulation of painful secrets, well and proudly kept. Kept because there is no comfort in the telling, no release in the revelation.

Faadumo crept into the room. "Assia, Assia?" she whispered.

"Yes, Faadumo."

She took my hand in that unspoken gesture of affection and understanding between women. "They're coming," she warned. "I heard them stirring and I raced to get here before them."

"It's fine, Faadumo," I said to reassure both her and myself. Faadumo and I sat in the gathering light and waited expectantly for the women, much like we had waited for mother to return with some milk, or the trade truck to arrive when we were little. I had no secrets then, and showed my feelings on my face. Now my face was as closed as my body was open.

The women entered the room like a lioness returning to her den, sniffing the air to find out what has occurred in her absence.

My mother-in-law approached me. "Are you well, new little sister?" she said. She had the air of one who thinks she has a right to do something and will not be deterred.

"Yes, mother," I said.

She drew the bedclothes away from my body and inspected the freely flowing blood between my legs. *"Saah,"* she exclaimed loudly, clicking her tongue against the top of her mouth in an expression of satisfaction. The room exploded into a wild frenzy of ululation and dancing. Faadumo whirled about the room clapping her hands and singing the loudest of anyone. "Now you are a woman, now you have kept your promise, a strong and beautiful Somali woman. Allah grant you many children."

They woke the village up with their singing and ululation running through the town in triumph. A promise had been kept. I wondered where Hajji had gone and when he would return to me.

Hassan
N'asse

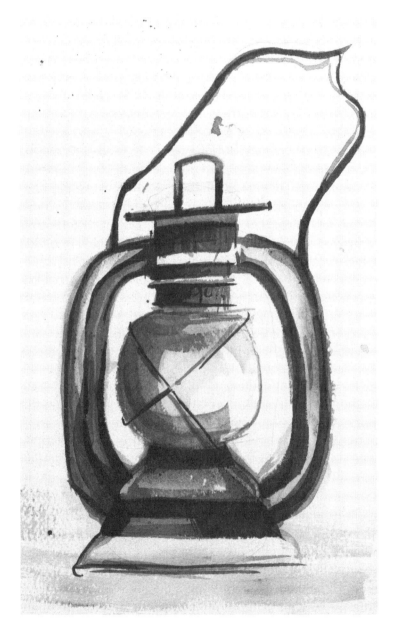

*Righteous is he who believeth
in Allah . . .
and giveth wealth, for love of
Him,
to kinsfolk and to orphans
and the needy and the way-
farer . . . .*

—Sura 2:177, The Cow

Hassan N'Asse was the village fool.
He was unable to care for himself and so
he was taken care of by the villagers in
turn. He wandered around the market
place in the morning and mumbled and
hummed to himself. He was always present at any community activity and was
allowed to stay no matter how solemn
the occasion. He was considered as
much a part of village life as the elders
or the beautiful women. He belonged to
God along with everything else in the
world and his behavior was a fulfillment
of God's will. The people of Arabsiyo
accepted him and their duty towards
him. He gravitated to whatever caught

his eye, anything that shifted, smelled, or shouted. One day Chamis saw him walking in a circle on her way home from selling pots in the market.

"Hassan, you are filthy, you come home with me," said Chamis. Hassan had been sitting in the pile of garbage at the edge of the little open air market and he was filthy. He smelled of the rotten oranges and putrid papaya thrown away by the farmers during the morning hours of the market. He could have been a handsome man, he had fine, evenly spaced features, and his body was well proportioned, but his vacant stare and slack jaw revealed serious problems. Hassan had come to the garbage pile to find something he had lost, but he could not remember what he was looking for when he got there. He sat all morning sifting garbage between his fingers and singing softly to himself. The truth was, that Hassan was lost, lost in an inner world that had nothing to do with reality. He liked to feel the soft old fruit and smell the odors. He imitated the sounds of the goats let loose to forage in the garbage. He was oblivious to the hot sun baking the bits of fruit to his skin like the crusted edges of rice left in a dish.

"Hassan, get up out of the garbage and come with me," repeated Chamis.

Hassan remembered Chamis, he recognized her voice among the others that wandered around the misfiring connections in his mind. He knew that she would not hurt him and he remembered that he was hungry and thirsty. He got up out of the garbage and followed her willingly through the dusty streets of the little town to her house, like a small boy eager to please his mother. Chamis was a tall woman and she moved her body gracefully. She swayed her backside as she balanced her collection of pots on her head. Chamis had light skin and fierce black eyes. She wore bright colors and knew as she passed the tea shop that the men watched as she walked by.

Chamis made Hassan sit on the stone step in the front of her whitewashed mud-brick house. It was located not far from the tea shop and the *quat* market where the man spent many hot afternoons. Hassan picked at the skin on the back of his hand and muttered to himself while she went inside. Soon five little boys saw him sitting there and gathered across the street. They threw little stones at Hassan to get his attention, afraid to come too close to him. He picked up the stones and talked to them as if they were his precious pets.

"Oh, my sweetie, *habibe*, looky, looky, looky, *habibe*," he said between puckered lips, to the great amusement of the children. He seemed oblivious to their presence and played with one after the other of the stones.

"Oh, my, oh, my," he said laughing up at the sky for no reason, with a sound like the crazed call of the hyenas that roamed the empty streets late at night. Hassan the Fool had his own reasons. He wandered throughout the town, he often did not know his name, but he was usually harmless and was a member of the Saad Musa tribe. He was related to many of the townspeople and had assumed a place at the bottom of the social pecking order. The person at the bottom is just as important as the person at the top in establishing the order of those in between. The villagers had nicknamed him, affectionately, *Hassan N'Asse*, Hassan the Fool, for that he was. He wandered about the quiet streets too confused to even beg. He was like a little child, despite being over six feet tall and perhaps twenty-five years old. He would not look for food or clean himself if someone did not bring him home and tell him to do it. He usually caused no harm to anyone, except for frightening the little children when he screamed or barked like a wild animal. Over the years, the villagers had rather gotten used to his odd behaviors. It was the will of Allah, they said, Hassan had no will of his own.

It is the sacred duty of a Muslim believer to take care of the poor, and Hassan N'Asse was certainly needy. He had only the ragged shirt and *ma'aweiss* that he wore. He had no other earthly possessions, and no thoughts that would direct his mind toward a goal. His thoughts twisted and turned in his mind, distracted by every color or smell his body encountered, like a little bit of fluff tossed about at the whim of the wind. He belonged to Allah and the villagers took turns caring for him. Many believed that Hassan was spiritually protected by God and injury to him would bring divine retaliation. According to ancient unquestioned traditions, the blessing or curse of the helpless was considered especially potent because the power of a person to do injury is proportionate to their helplessness. Many in the village were wary in his presence and warned the children to stay away from him. This reinforced the power of the feeble in the minds of another generation.

Chamis returned with a basin of water and a little piece of soap. She shooed the children away, but they ran behind the adjoining house to watch the fun. What else is there to do in a quiet little village?

Chamis made Hassan take off his filthy shirt and *ma'aweiss*. She handed it to her daughter Zahara to wash. Zaraha was fifteen and had the same light skin and coal black eyes as her mother. Tomorrow was Friday and all the men of the village would go to the mosque at noon for prayers. Hassan always followed the men into the mosque, and imitated them in the *salat*. He had been beaten when he disrupted the services and had learned to be still and to follow whatever the others did. Chamis, like other women, was not allowed into the mosque, but she loved and respected the holy religion of Islam. It would be insulting to Allah to have Hassan N'Asse smelling up the place and distracting everyone from the words of the holy Quran. Chamis prayed by washing the village fool.

Hassan sat on the ground like a wayward child as Chamis washed him. He laughed and shouted at the tin roof when it caught his attention and shook his head when she wanted him to bend down so she could wash his hair. "Ahhhhhhhhh," he wailed, like a baby, but without emotion, without tears. Who knew what *jinn* had gotten into Hassan and taken away his mind? What had taken over his perfectly healthy body so that he could not function? It must have been a spirit.

"Hassan, hold still, you'll waste the water," said Chamis sharply.

"Ahhhhhhh," replied the naughty child.

The boys at the side of the house were howling with laughter to see this grown man act like a baby and stand naked before a woman. Chamis warned them to go away or the *jinn* would catch them and put voices inside their heads too. This shushed the children and they watched in silence. They peered around the corner of the house hoping to catch a sight of the *jinn*, while Hassan was being taken care of by an adult and it was safe.

Hassan moaned into the air. He would not lower his head and let her wash his filthy hair. Well, then he would just have to be that way, decided Chamis. "If you won't sit still Hassan, you are just going to be dirty." He laughed in agreement, nodding and smiling at her.

"Hassan," he said, pointing to himself and catching her eye. The brief encounter was difficult for him to sustain and he retreated to his inner world.

"Hassan, you fool," said Chamis, "what were you doing sitting in the garbage like the goats?"

"Hassan," he said slowly and carefully, pointing to himself.

"I want you to stay out of there, or no dinner. Do you understand me?" Chamis said sternly, knowing he could or would not understand.

"Hassan," was all he said, picking at the skin on the back of his elegant hand. His fingernails were long and curved because he never had occasion to break them.

Once he was clean, Chamis brought him inside her house. He sat quietly in the open courtyard that afternoon. Zahara washed his shirt and *ma'aweiss* and hung them outside on the branches of an acacia tree to dry. She shouted at the little boys who still hovered nearby, "Don't you touch this or I'll tell Hassan. He'll tell the *jinn* to get you too." Some of the boys were doubtful about the evil *jinn*, they were wearing amulets for protection, but they knew that Zahara would catch them for sure, and they left Hassan's clothes alone.

Chamis cooked the afternoon meal for herself and Zahara. She made rice with a little goat meat and tomato sauce over the charcoal cooking stove. Hassan sat outside in the courtyard, humming to himself and playing with bits of straw from the mat he sat on. When she and Zahara finished, Chamis fed Hassan what was left of the dinner. She had been careful to leave some nice bits of meat for Hassan but Zahara, ravenous as usual, had eaten almost everything and complained about feeding a fool.

Hassan ate eagerly, he grabbed big handfuls of the rice and stuffed them into his mouth. He did not care that he had bits of food all over his chin and around the edges of his face. He did not feel his own body, he certainly did not feel the conventions of good manners. When all of the rice was gone, he sucked on his fingers loudly, one by one. Zahara sulked inside the house at this display of ignorance. When his shirt and tattered *ma'aweiss* were dry, Chamis helped him to dress. She hated filth and could not stand it when Hassan walked around the village dirty. He backed out of the house bowing as he went. He had been hungry and Chamis was glad she had fed and bathed him. She had done many things in her life that were forbidden by the teachings of Mohammed and she was ready to atone for her sins by acts of charity. Chamis had been widowed, then divorced by two husbands. She had been tossed outside the boundaries established for proper Somali women. She supported herself and her daughter and slept with whomever she pleased. Flickering fears of divine punishment for her actions emerged from the edges of her mind during times when she was discouraged or being snubbed by village women. Taking care of Hassan N'Asse was a way to assuage her guilt. It was God's will that he could not take care of himself, that he had no mind, no sense. Chamis gave what she could to Hassan for the sake of fulfilling God's will. He needed to be fussed over, to be fed, and talked to gently. He was not very different from other men in these simple needs, he did not frighten her. She was without the protection of a husband and an extended family; she understood helplessness. When she cared for Hassan she cared for her own fears.

"*Nabad, nabad,*" he said waving at the children as if they were old friends instead of mischievous little boys.

"*Nabad gelyo*, Hassan," said Chamis. She, of all the villagers knew what it was to be hungry, to be frightened and alone in the world. She had a special place in her heart for Hassan. The prophet Mohammed had taught that when gifts of charity are given to the needy, the giver benefits as well as the receiver. Washing Hassan was a way for Chamis to purify her own soul.

Hassan took to sitting under a big tree on the outskirts of town. It was next to the road to Hargeisa and near the place where the weekly trade truck stopped to load and unload cargo and passengers. He began to act as if this were his private tree and to chase the children away when they came to tease him. He hung little scraps of paper brought from the marketplace on the branches. He jumped up and waved the trade trucks away from the tree as they came up the road into town. He stood in front jumping up and down and yelling, "Get away, get out of here." The trucks never came near the tree, but followed the road that ran beside it, leaving Hassan standing there, waving frantically at the desert to stay away. He howled at the cloud of dust stirred up by the truck's tires and cursed it.

Hassan usually wandered into the *suuq* during the day. He picked up little pieces of paper or shreds of plastic or bits of cloth from the refuse pile in back of the market. Sometimes he would be attracted to a bit of paper still holding tea leaves in one of the stalls. Hassan would approach the unguarded merchandise and grab the colorful paper. Holding his precious prize, he would run off, chased by the angry merchant who had been left with his tea spilled all over the ground and wasted.

Hassan the Fool hung the colored papers on the tree's limbs, often crawling painstakingly into the tallest branches. One day he fell out and hit his head, but it did not knock any sense into him. He continued to decorate the poor tree bit by bit with little pieces of paper, tiny strips of cloth, and worn out plastic bags.

The tree began to look like an upright garbage pile it was hung with so many tatters of this and that, all waving in the wind. If something got torn off in the breeze, Hassan would scamper after it into the desert, calling it as if were a lost goat wandering into danger. He had to be very hungry to leave the tree to come and get something to eat. The more refuse he put on the tree, the more distracted Hassan was. His mind was caught up in the waving paper flags. He lay on his back under the tree looking up. His mind was caught and began to twist and turn like a kaleidoscope. Each patchwork mosaic that his optic nerve delivered to his brain, caused new perseveration and he could not escape.

"Hassan, I can see that you haven't eaten today. You come with me now," said Chamis. Hassan was lying under the tree staring up into the whirling, turning papers on the branches. The colors were melting together and sighing, the tree was alive. He was beginning to look a little wild, fierce determination had replaced the vacant stare.

"My tree, Somali tree," said Hassan N'Asse pointing at his magnificent creation. The ground underneath was littered with bits of garbage Hassan had not yet put on the tree. He was so distracted by the living, breathing tree that he could not even remember to decorate it anymore.

"Hassan, come home with me."

"Tree."

"Hassan, let's go have some food."

"No." He had turned and hugged the trunk of the tree, defying her to come and touch him, like a two-year-old having a temper tantrum. Hassan held the solid bark of the tree's trunk and felt it respond to his embrace. His knees felt weak from the power he held in his arms. He placed his face next to the roughness and rubbed. Electricity ran through his body and he sank to his knees, overcome with the sensation.

Chamis left shaking her head, Hassan was becoming weak and more disoriented than she had ever seen him. Later than afternoon, she sent Zahara with a tin plate of rice left over from their meal. Zahara had walked up under the tree and ignored Hassan when he yelled at her. "Oh shut up, you stupid goat," she said, angry that she had not seen a certain young man when she passed near the quat market. She had no patience for this silly fool and his fluttering tree. She held the plate out to him, shaking it under his nose as he struggled to stand up while holding on to the living trunk. Hassan flung his arms out, flailing at the air. He hit the plate and the rice was thrown up and all over Zahara. She was furious, she had to walk all the way back through town, past the *quat* market, covered with rice. Of course, everyone stopped and watched her rage by; there were few secrets in Arabsiyo.

"Let that fool starve if he wants to," she shouted at her mother. "He is useless and ought to die. Why do we feed people who are too stupid to even eat? Let him work like the rest of us." Zahara was meticulous about her dress, it was her only one and she hated when anything got on it. Now she had to wash it and there was no clean water left in the jug. She had to wear Chamis's other dress while hers was left to dry. The light dress was made to be cool in the heat of the day, and it dried quickly, but Zahara held on to her anger all that afternoon.

"You made me take the rice to that stupid idiot," she said to Chamis. Zahara just wouldn't leave the incident alone, she shook the charcoal stove so hard the handle came off. "Everyone saw him throw it at me, how could you do that to me!" she wailed. Finally Chamis promised to buy her another dress as soon as she had enough money. Chamis wondered if she would see the District Commissioner from Gebulay during the week, he often came to stay the night with her and was generous when he came.

The next day, Hassan attacked a small boy who, like Zahara, had come too near the tree. The baby had wandered away from his mother while she was shopping in the market. Probably the boy had been attracted to the magical, rippling tree. Hassan had been sleeping or lost in his mind's maze of pulsating paper and did not see the little boy until he was standing right under the tree, staring at it. Hassan had leapt up, howling, and actually thrown the poor child right out into the road, like a half-empty sack of grain. Fortunately the baby had not been physically hurt, only frightened by the baying, barking madman. Men from the market had come out and beaten Hassan with their sticks. He had retreated under his tree like a mother dog protecting her puppies and barked all afternoon, blood from the blows running down his face. He was too crazy to even wipe off his cheek and the blood dried down one side of his face with bloody bits on the nose and chin. His eyes had changed from limpid pools of empty black to angry slits. He was hoarse from thirst, but he would not stop barking at the bits of garbage stirred up by the wind in the night. He was beginning to frighten the children and the more superstitious souls in the town.

Chamis had gone to the tree after dark with a plate of food and a cup of water. He had snarled and howled as if he did not recognize her at all. She left the plate and cup a little distance from the tree, but Hassan did not hear voices that told him he was hungry or thirsty. His inner demons would not allow him to see or feel anything but them.

Several of the village elders, and those who considered themselves elders, gathered that night in Ali Yare's store to discuss the situation. The harsh glare of the two Tilly lanterns silhouetted the chiseled features of the old men and made the eyes of the younger men glisten.

"He should be killed," said Ibrahim. "He is dangerous and only causes trouble in town." He drummed with his fingers on the wooden counter polished with the oils of many hands as he talked. He was a young man with carefully groomed hair and he smelled of toilet water. Despite the care he took with his clothing, his teeth still held little bits of green from the *quat* he had chewed that afternoon.

"Hassan is mad according to God's will," responded Ali Yare quietly. "We are not going to kill him." He looked over at Ibrahim, and the subject of murder was closed. Ali Yare had more authority in a wave of his hand than other men had holding a gun. He was a devout Muslim and had endeared himself to the members of the community with quiet acts of strength, compassion, and kindness. He was short of stature, hence the nickname, Ali the Little, but he was long on authority.

"Put him on a truck to Hargeisa then, he can beg in the city."

"Beg? Hassan doesn't know how to beg," said Subti,

who was respected as one of the teachers at the school. Everyone laughed, and the tension dissolved into the moonless night sitting just outside the door.

"He is Saad Musa, we can't just send him away," said Hajji Omar, another elder. He wore the round embroidered hat of one who has made the holy pilgrimage to Mecca. Hajji Omar fingered his well-worn prayer beads as he spoke.

"Why not?" asked Ibrahim, "The Issaq just put them out in the desert if they can't take care of themselves."

"I hear there is a hospital in Hargeisa for the insane," offered Subti.

"That is not our tradition, these hospitals. It is our duty to care for the helpless," repeated Hajji Omar.

There was no easy solution to the problem. The men talked far into the night and did not decide what to do.

Chamis was glad to see that the tin cup of water had been emptied during the night when she stopped by the tree early the next morning. She was on her way to her stall in the market where she sold cookware to support herself and her daughter. Hassan sat under the canopy of his magic tree and cried to himself. When she tried to come closer to him, he started to snarl right in her face and she quickly withdrew. Chamis saw that someone else had left a plate of *lahough*, the morning pancakes, for Hassan. Like the rice she left the previous evening, they were untouched. Probably Amina, she thought. Amina was Ali Yare's daughter-in-law. She often fed Hassan and saw that he was clean. Chamis thought that Amina would know what the elders had discussed the previous evening, and decided to watch for her in the market that morning.

All that day the talk about Hassan continued. The men discussed him as they sat in the tea shops, the women talked in the courtyards of the houses where they worked, and in the market where they went to shop. Some people said he had gone crazy because of his love for his cousin.

Many years ago when Hassan was almost grown to his full size, he had followed his first cousin, Assia, around for months, talking of his love for her, making quite a pest of himself. Assia was lively, bright, and the most beautiful girl in the village; she humored Hassan but the whole thing was ridiculous. Her father was powerful and would arrange a good match for her, there was no way she would have anything to do with silly Hassan. Finally, her brother, Ibrahim, had told Hassan to stop bothering her, there was no chance of a romance between them. He had kicked Hassan viciously to get him away from the house.

Hassan had become very strange after that, and it was feared that a *gelid* or spirit had gotten into him because of this unrequited love. A *gelid* usually caused very crazy behavior when it got into people, and it entered people who were weak and unhappy. His grandmother had arranged for a *wadaad* or medicine man to read from the Quran and command that the gelid leave Hassan. Despite these measures, the spirit remained in possession of Hassan's mind and would not leave him.

Hassan had continued to live in his own little world, rocking and singing to himself. Assia had married and gone away to live in Hargeisa. When she came to visit her family, he did not even recognize her.

Other people claimed that Hassan had been strange even as a young baby. He had recoiled at his mother's touch, he arched his back and cried when he was picked up. His mother had finally left him in the *aqual* because he struggled so much when she tried to carry him on her back. He spent his childhood rocking back and forth and singing softly to himself. He had never gone to Quranic school or played with the other children. He had stayed at home next to his mother's skirts, until she died. He had gone to live with his cousins, but had started to bite himself. He soon had open sores all over his arms. Finally his cousin Abdi hit him with a stick whenever he bit himself. Hassan would bite and hurt himself, but he did not like it when other people hurt him. He had stopped the biting. His father could not take him into the interior to tend the livestock because he wandered off and did not stay with the animals. Someone had to go and find him, off in the desert somewhere singing to the clouds. He was worse than useless and only caused endless trouble with the animals. Eventually his family gave up and he ended up wandering around the village.

That day, a crowd of small boys gathered on the side of the road across from the tree and threw stones at Hassan unless someone chased them away. The little boys had dared each other to see who would be the first to touch Hassan and be the bravest boy in the village. Some of the boys were good shots and they often struck their mark. The target would run out shouting and throwing stones back at the boys. It was a crazy scene. Half the adults laughed to see the fool taunted by the babies, others worried that Allah would bring divine punishment on those who dared to mock the helpless. They shouted at the boys to go away, but they would not stay away from this devilish game for long.

Amina came to get her tin plate and she left a cup of water for Hassan. She saw Chamis in the market when she went to buy some oranges and rice for the afternoon meal. "Chamis," she said, "was that your cup and plate in the road by Hassan N'Asse?"

"Yes, I think he found the water, but the birds got the rice before he did."

"I last saw him eat at Omar's, on Friday afternoon," said Amina. "He listens to Hajji Omar and to Ali Yare but he won't hear me anymore." Amina did not know when Hassan had eaten after that and neither did Chamis. She decided to go to her father-in-law's store.

"Father, give me a tin of pineapple for Hassan N'Asse. He won't eat what we bring, but I know he loves pineapple."

"Pineapple, when did Hassan have pineapple?" asked Ali Yare. Everyone in the store was laughing at her request for a delicacy to feed a fool.

"I gave him some of what was left over after the American teacher visited," replied Amina. "Hassan liked it very much." She could understand the laughter. Pineapple was an expensive dish for a fool who didn't have enough sense to even eat.

"When he gets hungry enough he'll eat." The comment came from the back of the room, and was followed by more laughter.

"So," mused Ali Yare, "Americans and mad-men like tinned pineapple." He knew that many in the village felt there were other similarities between the woman from a strange land and the Somali with a strange mind. He handed her the tin with a smile at his thoughtful daughter-in-law.

Amina stood at the edge of the tree and called to Hassan. He was crying and mumbling to himself. "Hassan, listen to me," she said.

He was a frightening sight with dried blood on his face, dirty, unshaven, and thin. He glared at her.

"I have a present for little Hassan," coaxed Amina, holding the pineapple out so he could see it.

"Hassan," said the mad man, and he pointed to himself.

"Yes, you are Hassan N'Asse," repeated Amina calmly. She placed the open tin of pineapple on the ground and backed away. She squatted down and held her hand up to her forehead in order to block the sun and watch what he would do. Hassan crawled out from under the tree and took the tin. He ate the pineapple like a hungry lion, in big gulps.

"Hassan," he said quietly to her, pointing to himself. He licked the sweet juice off his dirty fingers, sending a shiver up Amina's spine. She hated dirt and uncleanliness. Seeing Hassan unmindful of his filthy fingers bothered her more than his howling.

That night the discussion about the town's fool continued in Ali Yare's store. "He is ruining a perfectly good tree. We don't have many trees, he should be chased away from that tree."

"Ha, we used to sit and talk about our problems under that tree before Hassan made it such a mess."

"He should be beaten until he cleans it up."

"When he is under the tree, we know where he is. If you chase him away, he may grab other children, or the baby goats."

"Ha."

"Hassan has never grabbed any goats, he doesn't have that much sense."

"Amina said he ate some pineapple today," said Ali

Yare.

"Great, we can just beggar ourselves to feed him pineapple."

"The Quran does not ask us to give what we do not have. Why shouldn't we act charitably toward this poor soul and protect him from harm?" said Hajji Omar, reminding every one of the third pillar of Islam, almsgiving.

The elders were hard pressed to decide how to deal with Hassan again that night. He had wandered off when told to watch the livestock. He would not stand in the fields and crack a whip to keep the birds out of the ripening grain. He was useless, but when left on his own for too long, he began to see and hear what was inside his head. He lost more and more contact with what was really happening. Arabsiyo was not a community with the surplus to care for someone forever.

Hajji Omar's son, Mohammed Omar, got up to leave the little gathering. He had strong, well-defined muscles developed in long hours of work. His face was smooth and unburdened with the troubles of the men who lived in town and worried about money. Mahammed Omar was a poor man, and he had a peaceful soul. He owned a little orchard on the other side of the *tuug* and could not leave the orange and lemon trees for long, they were heavy with fruit and had to be watched each night. "I wish Hassan would sleep under my trees and keep everything away from my fruit," he said with a smile.

Well, that was an idea, thought Ali Yare as Mohammed shuffled out the door in his paper thin *da'as*. If Hassan guarded the tree littered with paper, would he guard the trees ripe with fruit in the orchards? Would he attack Mohammed Omar when he came to harvest the fruit? Could he be made to understand that he needed to guard the trees from everyone but Mohammed Omar?

The next morning Ali Yare and Hajji Omar went to the tree outside of town. Hassan was biting his arm and crying to himself. He stopped and stood up when he saw the two old men. He waved back and forth as if he were a mother rocking a fretting child on her hip. The two elderly friends stood in the road watching Hassan for a long time. Often the will of Allah was hard to understand.

Finally, Ali Yare had seen enough. "Hassan, come with me," he said. Few refused a direct command from Ali the Little. Hassan pointed at himself.

"Hassan," he whined. He picked at himself, and dropped his head down between his shoulder blades and followed the two men slowly through the village. The small boys stayed out of sight, they knew better than to disrupt the elders. Ali Yare told Amina to bathe Hassan and give him some dinner. He told Hassan to sit on the mats in the courtyard and to do whatever Amina told him. Hassan was still, he looked like a prisoner waiting to be punished. He did not move when Amina bathed his cut head, and washed the dried blood baked onto his skin. He held his body perfectly still and rigid. While she worked with this practically immovable man, Amina thought that he seemed to swing between two extremes of behavior. Either he was passive and childlike, doing whatever anyone told him with total innocence, or he gradually got violently wrapped up into something and became aggressive and ferocious. He could not tolerate either sort of behavior for long and would swing back into the other ways of behaving over time.

In the lull of the late afternoon, when the villagers began to stir after chewing *quat* or resting, Ali Yare took Hassan out to Mohammed Omar's orchard. The gardens were located on the other side of the dry river bed. This river flowed only after a rain. At night during the rainy season, it was often filled with dead branches and other debris that had been washed into it during the tremendous power of the late afternoon thunderstorms. The raindrops in these storms were large and heavy, they sounded like stones being poured on the tin roofs of the houses. The rainstorms blew up suddenly and lasted only for an hour or so, but the intensity of the showers was often dangerous. The drops were painful on bare skin like giant hailstones and the *tuug* changed into a raging torrent of water in seconds. Occasionally there would be a storm in a distant part of the interior, unseen in Arabsiyo. Suddenly a wall of water would come roaring down the *tuug* and unsuspecting cattle or goats would be washed away in the torrent. Children were warned to stay away and not to play in the sandy bottom of the *tuug*. Trucks hurried down one side and up the other to keep from getting stuck in the sand and swept away by a sudden rush of water. During the rains, the *tuug* usually ran during the night and was dry in the morning. The gardens were located on the other side of the *tuug* from the town. But it was necessary only once or twice a year to wade across the water. The *tuug* was usually dry again by mid-morning.

The *tuug* was dry that afternoon, it had not rained for several days and Hassan walked behind Ali Yare humming and singing to himself. He liked the orchards and all the trees, his belly was as full as his mind was empty. Mohammed Omar's orchard was fenced by acacia branches piled high and wide. The thorn fence kept most of the animals out, but not the birds or human predators. Mohammed had built a little shed for his tools and himself. He slept there to guard his gardens and to save money because he wanted to get married. He was getting older and needed to put together some money for a bride price. It was late in the day, after the sun had finished baking the place, and Mohammed was irrigating his garden. He would never waste water by irrigating during the day. The precious water would only evaporate off the plants in the heat of the day. Mohammed waited until the late afternoon when the water would do the most good.

He had an elaborate system of irrigation. He had a gasoline pump bringing up water from the deep well he had dug with his brothers. The water went down a main canal until it reached the end of the row. Mohammed made an indentation with his bare foot to allow the water to run into the square depression around the plants. When the depression had filled with water, he stopped up the opening, and made another opening in the plot across the row. This required proper footwork and timing almost like an elaborate ballet. Mohammed continued his delicate dance all down the first row and into the second, third, and fourth.

Mohammed did not joke or chatter while he was watering his fields. This was important work with a precious commodity and he concentrated. His face was smooth and his eyes had the clarity of one who is at peace with himself. He was glad for the water, for the feel of the smooth mud between his toes, and he rejoiced in the miracle of his gardens.

Hassan N'Asse sat on the ground when Ali Yare sat on the low stool Mohammed brought out of the shed for him. He had a cup of the tea Mohammed offered from his thermos. He picked at the skin on the back of his hands, but he did not bite his arm. Ali Yare and Mohammed talked softly, lulled by the sweetness of life in a garden before the harvest.

"This pump must make irrigation a lot easier."

"It's great when it works. These things have a mind of their own," said Mohammed.

"I hope that Hassan will stay put with you, I don't know what else to do with him."

"It's quiet out here, he won't here any voices telling him to decorate the trees. Mohammed tried to catch Hassan's eye, "Right, Hassan," he said, "no bits of paper."

"Hassan." Was the answer.

"Well," said Ali, "he's recognizing his name. When he forgets that, we will start having trouble with him."

When Ali got up to leave, Hassan started to follow him. Ali told him to stay with Mohammed. Hassan cried, and pointed to himself. "No," said Ali Yare firmly, "you stay here with Mohammed." Hassan would not disobey Ali. He stood under the orange tree rocking and crying like a lost child.

Mohammed Omar did not think this idea was going to work if Hassan kept him up all night with this crying. He brought Hassan some of the milk he had for the evening meal and Hassan was still. Mohammed gave him an old *goa* to wrap himself in when he slept. Hassan wrapped himself up as he saw Mohammed do and leaned against the tree. He looked as though he was waiting for Ali to come and take him back to the village.

Hassan stayed in the garden for several nights. He

guarded the trees and would not let anyone near them except for Omar. He slept during the day while Omar worked and wandered among the trees during the night. Omar's garden was isolated and the village was too far away for anyone to see it at night. When the moon was out you could see the minaret of the mosque from that side of the *tuug*, but when it was a new moon nothing of the sleeping town could be seen. One moonless night, Hassan wandered into the silent desert looking for something that he had lost. After darkness wrapped its bare arms around the gardens, there were no lights to give a sense of direction to a person without an internal one.

Chamis looked for him and walked around the little hills in back of the gardens all one afternoon. She could not get Zahara to come with her to look for Hassan. Zahara was still angry about her dress and the rice. She preferred to stay in town alone and Chamis worried about what she was up to. She asked her lover, the District Commissioner, to look out for Hassan when he drove his Land Rover on the road to Gebulay, but he was not sighted in that direction either.

The villagers never did find Hassan N'Asse and they wondered if he had been swept away by the rushing waters of the *tuug* or had gone to Hargeisa to learn how to beg. They knew that it was the will of Allah, the Merciful.

Chamis

*O death
may your name perish!
Though in truth
we are all on trek
Trudging in your direction...*
—Somali Poem by
  Cabdulqaadir Xirsi Yam Yam

During the languid afternoons
while the ravishing sun slowly continued her pre-determined travels over the
ginger desert, I sat in the shade and listened to my girlfriends tell the stories of
their lives. They described lives spent in
sheltered childhood, in hoping for love,
and in motherhood. These women were
carefully protected by fathers, brothers,
and kinsmen. They did not expect to
make many decisions about their lives
and were content to follow the path that
tradition had determined for them.
Chamis was the only woman in the village outside the protection of her tribe.
The other women gossiped and talked
about her but I wondered if they really
understood what motivates a woman
when she is truly alone.

She came to my house once, on the very first morning I stayed in Arabsiyo. She was bold enough to come right inside and see the white devil sleeping. After I was adopted by Amina and Ali Yare, she kept her distance. They were powerful people in the town, she was outside the network of proper Somali society. I only went to her house once. When her daughter committed suicide I went to pay my condolences. Chamis ignored my presence; the visit was an American custom, not a Somali one.

"Zahara, Zahara," Chamis wept and wrung her hands, but there was nothing for it but to sit helplessly by the side of the mat. Zahara was so badly burned she could not bear the slightest touch. Not even her hands were spared, she had spilled gasoline on them in her frantic pouring. "Why, oh why, did you do this?" her mother moaned. The lament of a mother who can no longer touch her child. However, this inability to touch did not start with this gasoline and fire. Zahara and Chamis had not touched in a long time. Chamis thought and thought about it, watching her only child die a horrible death. A death she chose. A mother remembers many things in a different way when she is sitting next to her dying child, unable to give the slightest comfort. Chamis had buried another baby, a boy, but it was not like this.

There is nothing in this life like the suicide of your own child. You always expect to bury your mother and father. This is as it should be, and you grow spiritually when you do this. If you are a child when your mother dies, you become older with every shovel of earth that covers her in the grave. If you are a married woman, your children, and all the children of your family, become more precious to you. When your mother is gone from your arms, you reach out and draw your children close to reinforce the intangible connection between mother and child. If your mother dies when she is old, hanging on to life, refusing to let go like the thorns of the acacia tree that catch on your dress, you are grateful to see what the end of life is like. She taught you how to take your first steps in this world, now she shows you how to take your last breath. These passages into the afterlife are gifts to the living, as well as the dead. Suicide is a meaningless theft of life, it has no gifts for those left behind. It leaves only unanswered questions to haunt the living. We are born with our fists closed and we come into this world crying. We die with our hands open accepting the will of Allah, the Merciful. We die when we have cried enough.

"Allah have mercy on my daughter," Chamis prayed. Zahara had no hands to reach for Allah to beg forgiveness for this great sin, only blackened stumps: her fingers had been fused in the heat of the fire.

The village women hung back from the bed in a little circle. Chamis could hear their murmuring. "Zahara will die soon, she cannot last the night."

"It will be a mercy."

"Allah take her before she suffers any more."

These women had always watched Chamis from the fringes of their houses, now they hovered near the door afraid of her sorrow. They did not understand Chamis, could not understand this suicide. These village women did what they were told by their mothers, by their fathers, by the elders, by their husbands. They were protected by their extended families and were not encouraged to have minds of their own. Their own will was buried in the folds of their skirts, it had been lost in the shimmering fabric of their sheltered lives.

Chamis' father divorced her mother before she was born. He had accused her of sleeping with another man and denied any parentage. Her mother had named her daughter Chamis, her only name because she had no father to give her a second name. If she had been a male child, her mother would have named her Hajji plus one of the names of the Prophet. She would have had two names despite the fact that no father claimed her. When boys are little, everyone knows they are bastards, but when they are older, strangers will think they earned the name Hajji by completing the holy pilgrimage to Mecca. They will be treated with the respect due to one who has completed this journey, the duty of Muslims at least once in their lives. Chamis was always known as a bastard.

"Ah, Chamis," her mother often said, "you are the most beautiful girl I every saw. Allah gave you this beauty because He loves you." She told her daughter that she would marry well and they would both be rich, *enshallah*.

Chamis' mother died when she was only as tall as a goat. The elders of her clan gave her to a clansman, Ali Hassan, and his three wives. They beat the child, all three of those women. She worked during the day and into the night, pounding the grain into flour, sweeping the floor, milking the goats, fetching water, fetching water, fetching water. The flour was never pounded fine enough, she spilled too much of the milk, and took too long bringing the water. There was always something that she hadn't done right. Once Ali Hassan's oldest son, Musa, stole one of the goats and sold it in town. He took the money and spent it on *quat* and a woman to have sex with him at a *garish*, or *quat* party with women. Everyone blamed Chamis for the missing goat and said that she was sleeping and not watching the animals closely. Musa lied about having taken it. No one believed the little girl, she was just a poor relation. Musa even bragged about his theft to Chamis, who hated him and spit in his milk when he wasn't watching.

Chamis had no new clothes like the other children for the celebration at the end of Ramadan, *Eid AlAllah*. She only had one old *dira* and that dress was torn and faded from working in the sun. Her dresses were always castoffs that had already been used for sleeping and then by the women when they menstruated. Chamis felt that beggars were treated with more kindness than she. She had to run and fetch a plate of rice for the poor, when her own belly was calling for food. She learned to sit in her place, in the corner of the compound, and listen and wait patiently. Soon, someone would drop a bead, leaving it in the folds of the bedclothes. It would slip into her hiding place. Everyone would be distracted by a goat caught in the thorn bushes that fenced in the compound, lovely pieces of meat, the best, would slip into her mouth. Wait quietly for your chance, she learned, it will come. Chamis used to watch the birds flying in the sky so free and quick. She longed to be able to fly away from her troubles as easily as they. To be so small no one bothered about you, no one could catch you. She prayed that Allah would punish these women— they never prayed, not even once a day. When they did pray it was a show or done so fast it was a joke. Arms flailing up and down, backsides bending so fast they looked like they were milking the cattle.

As soon as she began to menstruate, Chamis was married to an old man who was angry with everything. Ibrahim was not wealthy and he could only afford one wife. When his old wife died, there was no one to take care of him, so the elders offered Chamis. Ibrahim beat her with the bottom of his shoe. Everyone would watch, no one would help Chamis drag herself from the dirt to nurse her poor thin body. Ibrahim said Chamis stole, and it was true. Chamis stole food to eat, and money when she could. Chamis hated his pointed nose and crooked teeth, half black and the other half missing. He had legs like an ostrich and eyes like one too, round and beady. There was no soft place on his body.

Chamis hated when he came to her in the night on the sleeping mat and put his penis between her legs. "Put it in," he would hiss into her ear, unwilling to touch her vagina because he considered it impure. Her infibulation had been a quick job, the Midgann woman had hardly bothered with the skinny child. She had only pricked the clitoris and made one quick stitch for the infibulation, so Chamis was not tightly closed. Soon however, Chamis learned to hold herself closed and sometimes the dreaded penis would go limp. Ibrahim's legs twitched when he slept, and if he lay on the sleeping mats facing her, he would kick Chamis in his sleep. He snored with his gnarled hands curled into a fist, and when he jerked in his dreams, he struck her in the back. Chamis would crawl across the room and watch his open mouth and hear his snoring in disgust. She preferred the cold floor to his touch.

When the Yibir medicine man came to the village, Chamis had to beg and beg Ibrahim for the money to pay for an amulet to keep *jinn* away from the baby going inside her body. When Ibrahim finally relented and gave her five shillings, Chamis had to walk all the way to the next village to find the Yibir man again. The Yibir laid a small stick along his outstretched arm to the tip of the little finger. He touched his chin to the stick and recited holy incantations from the Quran in favor of the child.

"In the name of Allah, the compassionate, the merciful: Please grant us pardon, and forgive us. Allah have mercy on us. You are our protector; so help us against ungrateful people." His eyes rolled back in his head when he chanted so Chamis knew he was really a holy man, not just some fake. "In the name of thy Lord who createth, Createth man from a clot," he said. Chamis longed for the protection of Allah, there was no one else who cared. The Yibir medicine man inscribed the holy words from the Quran and other ritual signs on a bit of paper. He folded this into a piece of leather. Chamis tied this onto her arm to keep it close to the baby inside her body and gave the Yibir money for the blessings. It was not considered payment for his efforts, but an installment on the blood money owed to an ancestor of the Yibir, Mohammed Hanif. He had been killed in a contest of magic with the Somali Saint, *Au Barkhadle* (the Blessed One). Chamis knew that the power of the Yibir medicine men comes from a wind spirit that carries them away at the time of their death and was grateful to have his blessing.

Just before the birth of the baby, the village women gave Chamis a special party called a *falafala* to bless the child in her great belly and ensure an easy delivery. Again, Chamis had to beg and beg Ibrahim for a little money to buy frankincense and a bit of meat and rice to cook for the women. He was shamed into giving her the money but he sat outside the *aqual* during the dancing and singing for the baby, his child, like a spoiled child. The women were dancing for Chamis, but the father of the child sat outside pouting because Chamis was not bringing him his tea or rubbing his scrawny legs with oil.

When the time came to deliver the baby, the women dug a hole and lined it with soft cloth. They pounded two strong sticks firmly into the ground on either side of the hole and tied a strong cloth between them. When the baby water came gushing out of Chamis' body, Howa came to open the infibulation to allow the baby to be born. She was experienced and did the cutting during a contraction so Chamis would not feel the knife. The women helped her to crouch over the hole. It was all that day and into the next morning before the baby was born. Chamis was so weak from the long labor she could barely push the baby out into the soft hole.

Chamis sang many praises to Allah because her first born child was a boy. She took the sacred amulet off of her arm and hung it around his little neck. Although she had been angry because Ibrahim had given her only enough money to buy one small amulet, it looked enormous hanging on the baby's neck. It covered his entire little belly. She named the baby *Shiddeh,* or Painful One, because of the great difficulty he caused during his birth.

Ibrahim tried to come to sleep with Chamis soon after Shiddeh was born. Chamis screamed at him to stay away from her. The Prophet Mohammed had ordered that a woman cannot be touched by her husband for forty days after the birth of a child, but Ibrahim did not care. This is my right according to the holy Quran, Chamis screamed at him. On this point the others in the clan agreed with her, and Ibrahim was shamed into leaving Chamis alone. The old man did not even rejoice at the birth of a son in his old age. He grumbled about his tea and his rice. He wanted to be the baby and was jealous of his own son.

Ibrahim, according to Somali custom, allotted one she-camel for his new son. "Shiddeh," Chamis sang to her baby, "this navel-knot stock will grow into many large herds. You will be a rich man, a rich man, with more camels than you can count." Chamis promised Shiddeh that she would help him to care for all the beautiful animals so they would grow fat and reproduce. Chamis loved that little baby. He was the first thing she ever had of her very own. Chamis prayed that he would love his mother and when he grew into a man he would protect her and plead her cause.

Ibrahim did not give Chamis any presents, or a new dress, or even any extra food or milk to reward her for producing a son. Chamis came to believe that he attracted an evil *jinn* into the house with his moaning about cold tea, his nasty temper, and his unkindness to the baby who was weak. The *jinn* are descended from Iblis, a spirit fallen from heaven, and are evil like all unbelievers. Chamis thought that Ibrahim enticed one right out of the desert. The goat milk spilled, the fire went out, baboons got into the compound and tore up the place, the rain leaked through the mats covering the *aqual*. It was all mischief caused by a *jinn*. That spirit haunted the *aqual* until it found the weakest member of the family, Shiddeh, and it got right into the child.

Suddenly the baby wouldn't nurse. "Your milk is sour," said the women. Chamis knew who was making her milk sour, it was that *jinn*. Ibrahim would not get the Yibir to come and call away the *jinn* no matter how much Chamis pleaded with him. He would not buy a fat goat and feast with the elders to pray and recite the holy Quran. They could have summoned the *jinn* and forced it to leave Shiddeh. He did nothing but sit in the sun on his three legged stool and blame Chamis for the baboons.

Chamis shaved Shiddah's sweet little head, but left a long piece of hair at the top. This is the "handle of Allah." Chamis left it in case this poor child should die, so Allah could reach down and pull him up to heaven by the handle. "In paradise the faithful are rewarded for their sacrifices on earth. There are golden pavilions and crystal streams in the garden of delights." Chamis told Shiddeh so he would not be afraid.

That baby boy died and Chamis believe he was murdered by his own father's unkindness. He was wrapped in a white shroud, the color of death and mourning and buried with the amulet still covering his whole little belly. The men dug a grave for him according to Muslim traditions. It was a hole with a little shelf for the body. The baby was placed on the shelf facing Mecca. It was not a hard grave to dig. The rains had just begun and the ground was soft. It was a small grave, like the body of that sweet baby.

Ibrahim got sick later in the same year. He had a wheezing in his chest, and he coughed up blood. Chamis thought he had been entered by a *wadaddo* or wind-spirit, or perhaps it was that same *jinn*. The elders read the Quran and Chamis burned incense and bathed his body in the smoke, but Ibrahim coughed more and more. His grave was dug in the hard dirt, packed and dried out by the sun. The men complained that the ground was hard, Chamis thought it was hard like his heart.

Chamis stood alone on a little hill watching the men bury Ibrahim. The other women stood a little apart, murmuring about what would become of Chamis without a husband. Who would the elders find to take care of her? Chamis didn't care. She put a stone on Ibrahim's grave every time she passed it. Not a prayer to Allah, but a stone to keep him in his grave.

According to the *dumal*, or inheritance, a man's relatives have a responsibility to care for a widow. Women do not inherit the possessions and livestock of their husbands. These are divided up among the male children and relatives. Ibrahim's brothers were dead, so Chamis was given to another kinsman, Saad. Like Ibrahim, he was old, but he did not complain, he was silent. He sat for a few days looking out into the desert, uncomfortable in the *aqual*. He agreed to marry the woman, it was his duty, but did not wait the three months required before the wedding could take place to ensure that Chamis did not carry Ibrahim's child. Saad left to tend his camels in the bush with his other wives, and did not take Chamis with him. He left her to fend for herself, as best she could. Saad left Chamis with one old goat for milk, too old to reproduce. When Chamis complained to the elders that Saad had a duty to take care of her needs, they answered, "He did not marry you, we shall break the betrothal." "We shall find someone else." Chamis was beginning to understand that the elders never found anyone to take care of her, she was only a poor relation. They found someone who needed to be taken care of. Chamis decided she would not trust anyone to make decisions for her if she could help it. She had discovered that people don't make decisions that benefit another, they made decisions that are good for them.

Chamis decided to go to Hargeisa. She would beg if she had to. She sold the scrawny old goat that was the only inheritance allotted to her from Ibrahim. She packed up the few things that were hers and walked away from the circle of *aquals* and across the desert. "May gazelles be born in your houses because you have all turned to dust," she spat as she turned away from the little outpost. She walked all that day to the tea shop where the trucks stopped on their way to Hargeisa.

Chamis felt that Allah blessed her on the truck ride into Hargeisa. She saw a man smiling at her, and remembered what her mother had told her about her beauty. She instinctively lowered her veil away from her face and smiled back at him. She held the veil tightly in her white teeth and teased him with flashing ginger eyes. Ali Omar had the soft brown eyes of a baby gazelle, his pupils grew large when he looked at the beautiful young woman traveling all alone. They both silently blessed the prophet when the truck lost a tire in the desert. Everyone had to get off the truck and wait for the rest of the day and all during the night for the driver to walk into the closest town. He had to find someone with a new tire to fix the truck, and a way back out to the road.

It was during this long wait by the side of the truck, that she met her next husband, Ali Omar. Chamis shared the milk from her *dhill* with him they talked and sat together. Late that night in the deep desert darkness, they kissed. When the truck was finally fixed and rolled again, Chamis was in love. When they came into Hargeisa that next day, Ali took her to the Quadi. They made the ritual promises and were married. There was no bride price to be paid, no endless haggling. Chamis had placed herself outside of the protection and direction of her clan. She was free to do as she pleased.

Ali Omar's people hated Chamis from the first time she walked behind him into the compound. His first wife stood silently in the doorway her hands clenched into fists.

Ali talked to her for a long time. "Chamis will help you, she will cook and fetch the water."

"I don't need help from her," she replied. Nurah was great with child and her feet were swollen. She stayed in the other room of the house and did not come out into the courtyard for the rest of the day. There were two rooms in this house with a long passage in between them. Both opened onto an inner courtyard with a small kitchen and a long drop.

Chamis stayed in the bed the first morning, after Ali Omar had gone into town. Nurah would know that she was not going to be the servant in this house. Soon pots began to fly about the courtyard, and Nurah threw ashes at Chamis when she left the room to make water. Chamis snatched at Nurah and tore her *dira*. Nurah tried to scratch out Chamis' eyes. Someone ran to fetch Ali Omar to stop the fighting. When he returned Nurah complained that Chamis had ruined her dress and she must have a new one. He gave her the money to have a new dress made and she triumphantly stalked away into the market, forgetting all about her swollen ankles. She returned with cloth for a new dress the color of the first grass after the rains.

Chamis knew her rights and she demanded a new dress as well. The prophet commanded that all of a man's wives must be treated equally under the law.

"This is not a proper wife," shrieked Nurah. "She came from the desert, send her back to the desert."

"We can not afford to feed this extra person," cried Ali's mother. "Our cooking pots are empty half of the time." She threw one at Chamis for emphasis. "You are not rich enough to afford two wives, Ali," she squawked. The place was at war. Members of the clan agreed with Nurah: this second wife would bring no honor to the family.

Eventually Ali gave in to the crying that never stopped. He came to Chamis and told her that he was divorcing her. Without a clan to take her side there was nothing that Chamis could do. She had no mother to defend her, no clansmen to threaten Ali if he did this. Chamis knew where he buried his money. She had seen him dig up the little pouch when he went like a bitten hyena to give money to Nurah for the new dress. That night, Chamis dug up the little pouch, took the money, and left before the morning light came looking for mischief.

Chamis bought some cooking pots, lids, bracelets, and big metal spoons in the market. She wrapped them into a bundle she could balance on her head and took a truck into the village of Arabsiyo. Chamis knew she could sell what she had purchased in Hargeisa for more in a little village. The rains had been good and she had heard that the farms in this town were producing lovely fruits and vegetables. People will have money for new pots, Chamis thought to herself.

Chamis was sick on the truck, the rolling ride made her lose her morning meal. Chamis was pregnant, but she soon discovered that it is easier to take care of yourself than it is to try and convince another person they should consider your needs. Chamis soon had a little spot in the Arabsiyo market and she sold kitchen wares there each day. Her daughter was born in the village, and she was an easy birth. When Chamis took Zahara to Hargeisa, to show her to Ali, her father, he was not home. His mother and first wife greeted her with insults.

"Get out of here you whore, you thief."

"This is not our relative."

"You cannot claim lineage to our clan. Allah knows who the father of the child is."

"We don't need a prostitute in the house. Take that girl away."

Chamis knew Ali Omar was a weak man and would never stand up to his mother, or his wife. She left with tiny Zahara on her back and bought more pots and cooking spoons in the large market in Hargeisa. Chamis stayed that night and made love with the Saudi merchant who sold the pots and she fed her daughter well to keep her from crying. The Saudi gave her twenty shillings for her kisses, and a very good deal on the pots. This relationship continued for many years; Chamis would come into Hargeisa, buy more wares to sell from the Arab, spend the night with him, and return to Arabsiyo on the truck.

Chamis kept Zahara with her in the market when she was little. She slept in the shade of her mother's baskets during the late morning. Chamis made her be silent so she would not disturb any haggling with the customers. If men came to Chamis in the night, she ignored the baby's crying and Zahara soon learned to stop. Chamis put a small oiled rag into her vagina to keep from becoming pregnant. She would urinate right after intercourse to keep any child from catching hold inside her body. She had a good living from her little business, but she needed a husband, not another baby.

Chamis thought that Zahara was a good girl when she was little. She would bring her mother tea and carry out the old ashes and dump them in back of the house. She learned to wash the clothes and lay them on the bushes to dry in the sun. She had plenty to keep her busy.

Chamis was often lonely with only Zahara for company. She had no family and the other village woman would have nothing to do with her. Sometimes she would bring Hassan N'Asse, the village fool, home with her and give him some food to eat. He was crazy and he would sit in the garbage pile in the market until someone called him away. Chamis was sorry for Hassan. Like her, he was an outcast. He had lost his mind, she had lost the protection of a lineage, of a family.

Over the years Chamis got to know the truck drivers because she went into Hargeisa every month or so to replenish her stocks. Sometimes, if it had not been purchased, they would offer her a seat in the truck's cab on the way back to Arabsiyo. She joked and talked about business and politics. Chamis was a woman on her own and knew as much as they did about such things.

One day Chamis shared the cab with the District Commissioner who lived in the next town along the road, Gebulay. He was a handsome man with his beige uniform and hearty laugh. Chamis felt it was wonderful to hear a ringing laugh filling up the whole cab of the truck. It was a piece of life Chamis wanted, this laughter. Chamis was pretty because she had been getting nice and fat, a coveted sign of beauty among the Somali. She felt confident with her round cheeks and big buttocks. Her money was going to feed her own belly, not anyone who thought they owned her. She tossed her head scarf back from her face and chatted with this handsome stranger. She was not a shy empty-headed village girl.

The D.C. joked with Chamis and found her stall in the market where he bought a new spoon for his wife.

"If my wife doesn't make better food, I shall use this to beat her, " he said. "Is it strong?"

"Anything I have is strong enough for you," Chamis answered, meaning something else.

Chamis asked after the D.C. in the town. She was told that he had been educated in Aden and had an educated wife, Ibado. The women gossiped about this wife. She was away, as she often was, visiting with her family in Aden. She did not cook or take care of his animals but demanded they have servants to do this work. She did not consider her proper duties as a wife of the district commissioner, but spent her time reading books and having her friends over for tea. She spoke English as well as Arabic, and complained that Gebulay was a boring outpost. She didn't care about the duty of a wife to support her husband, to tend his livestock, and ensure that the herds would grow. She did not care to bring him milk from the best goats, to bathe the house in incense when he came home. She was looking to teach in the girl's school, a woman with a husband and duties at home! This is what people told Chamis about the D.C..

Mohammed Abdi, the D.C., began to find Chamis in the market when he was in Arabsiyo. Chamis teased him about his educated wife.

"You are looking a little thin." she said softly and tilted her head so he had to draw near to her in order to hear. "What does this wife of yours cook that you can eat? Come to me tonight and I will make you a real meal of lamb and spicy rice. Your stomach will be grateful to you for this treat." Mohammed gave her five shillings, enough to buy food for a wonderful meal. Chamis hurried home to cook for him and think about his delicious laughter and his strong arms that wrapped all the way around her body.

Chamis sat while Mohammed Abdi ate and listened to his talk about the political situation. He said there were too many political parties and that everyone threatened to kill the winner of the election if it was not the candidate from their clan. "Chamis," he said, "we have to get beyond these tribal politics if we are ever to solve our problems. Everyone votes as many times as they can. Already the entire country knows that brake fluid will rub out the stamp they put on your hand to show that you voted." Mohammed shook his head.

"Yes," she laughed, "now everyone in town is trying to get more brake fluid than anyone else. Everyday they are in the market looking for brake fluid."

"Exactly, so they can erase the voting mark and vote again and again. This is ridiculous. The election will be decided on brake fluid, not anything to do with running the fool country."

"Mohammed," Chamis said, "If you don't let the people vote several times the aid we get from the United States and from the Russians will be cut. It's based on population estimates taken from voting patterns."

"Chamis, you are not only beautiful, but a very clever woman," he said. "I am tired of these silly girls who can't do anything but hide."

"And so what about your own wife?" Chamis asked him brazenly, baiting him.

"It was an arranged marriage, Chamis. She will be the mother of my children," he sighed, then took her hands and looked into her eyes. "Oh, Chamis, I need a woman like you," he said. "Someone who I can talk to. I need someone who will take care of me."

"So you expect me to give up my little business here in Arabsiyo and live like a prostitute outside your door?"

He laughed and pulled her close to him. Chamis loved his big laugh. His strong arms, his powerful position. No one dared to make fun of her in town any longer, he was a powerful man and she was his favorite. She felt safe in those unending arms of his, it was foolish, she knew, but she could not help it. Chamis longed for this feeling of protection, and the longing would not go away.

Mohammed's wife went to Aden again for a visit with her family. She wrote to say she would not return for several months until her sister had her baby. Mohammed came every Thursday to sleep with Chamis. Often he came in a Land Rover quite late in the night. Chamis could feel that he was lonely, sometimes she would turn and see the saddest look on his face. The servant girl stole him blind and cooked him food she bought cheaply in the market. She lied and told him it was more expensive. She took the buttons from his uniform and said they were lost. She left the cooking pots dirty so that cats came into the compound and howled, keeping him awake at night.

"Chamis," he said. "Come and take care of me. I am lonely."

"Marry me Mohammed, it's time you took a second wife to love, you have one for honor."

"Chamis, you know I cannot do that," was his answer. The D.C. could not marry an outcast, a known prostitute like Chamis.

Chamis taunted him, "What's the matter that you can't speak up to your family? You are more important that any of the old people. You are part of the new Somali. We are not nomads anymore, Mohammed. Nowadays people get married because they are in love, not to protect the tribe. You can just tell them what you want to do, they have to listen to you, you are the District Commissioner."

Then one day, Mohammed got very angry with some of the elders of his clan. They had insulted him at a *quat* party. They said he did not follow the old traditions and would suffer for it. His response was to come to Chamis and say that he was ready to take a second wife. Chamis was not a fool and quickly agreed.

They went to the Quadi at the Mosque that very day for the betrothal. Mohammed went back to Gebulay, and Chamis prepared for her wedding. Chamis decided to be the most traditional Somali wife in the entire village. No more insults in the marketplace for her. No more hot trips on the back of trucks guarding her little store of things to sell. Chamis would be a proper wife. She would cook and keep a good home for the District Commissioner.

Chamis had often dreamed of coming to Mohammed on her wedding night as a virgin, of starting her life over. She decided that she would have herself sewn up again like a young girl and go to him closed. Chamis would undo all of her former life and be a new virgin bride. This was her chance to start all over again, she would make Mohammed very happy. Chamis prayed to Allah and thanked him for this gift.

Zahara had become sharp tongued and critical as she grew into a young women. "Mother," she quarreled, "don't be a fool. Mohammed has slept here many times. How can he think you are a virgin just because you have yourself closed up?"

Chamis hit her with the bottom of her shoe. "Don't you ever, ever, talk like that to me again if you know what is good for you. Who is this I see you talking to in the market you little whore? If I find out you are with a boy you will fear to live, Zahara, when I finish with you."

Zahara sulked away, but Chamis knew she was seeing a young man in the town, she could see it in Zahara's careful arrangement of her head scarf when she went out. Once Chamis caught her daughter putting on eyeliner. That girl will never come to any good, Chamis thought.

The Midgann had taken great delight in the pain at Chamis' re-infibulation, she said the job had been botched the first time and she cut and cut until Chamis fainted. The bleeding would not stop for a long time, and it left her very weak and ill. Zahara wandered off instead of helping her mother. Chamis needed her to bring her tea and something to eat. Chamis could not move for fear of breaking open the stitches so painfully taken in her body. She lay alone in her bed and worried about her daughter and where she had gone.

"Zahara, where have you been all day?" Chamis raised up on one elbow.

"Out," was her answer.

"Zahara, I know about that boy you are seeing. He is a *quat* runner, you little fool. Surely you are not stupid enough to fall in love with an idiot who makes a living smuggling *quat* into the country." Chamis grasped Zahara's wrist and saw she had a new bangle. She grabbed it off and threw it across the room. "I will not have this, do you understand? This man will get you with a child and run off or get killed. He will never take care of you and you will be stuck with a bastard like I was with you."

Zahara wrenched herself away from her mother and left again. Back to her boyfriend, Chamis supposed, that little whore. She felt that her daughter did not appreciate the sacrifices she had made for her. Chamis wanted to protect her only child from a hopeless boyfriend, to keep her from the misery of her own life. Chamis wondered why Zahara didn't understand that. They had a chance to be respected. Chamis could find her a good husband with fine prospects with the D.C.'s help. Zahara, Chamis lamented from her bed, you little fool, why, oh why don't you realize what I am doing for you? She was really risking loosing it.

Mohammed came to visit Chamis and kissed her face. Chamis told him about her fears for her daughter and the description of the boy. Mohammed said he would see that the boy left town and would never return.

Zahara stayed home the week before her mother's wedding. She helped Chamis make a fine wedding dress and her mother bought her a new dress as well. Chamis wondered why her daughter looked up every time someone passed by outside the house. Chamis bought special frankincense to fill the room with a sweet smell on her wedding night and special foods to eat.

Zahara was critical as usual. "Mother, he is not providing you with your own house. He is bringing you to the very same house his first wife lives in. It's her house and you know it."

"So."

"So, what is going to happen when his first wife comes back? You are sleeping in her bed, using her cooking pots, her spoons and cushions. Do you think she is going to throw open her arms and welcome you? What do you think is going to happen?" she demanded.

"I am going to marry Mohammed, whether you like it or not," Chamis told her. "You are just jealous after that foolish boyfriend of yours ran off, just like I said he would."

Zahara gasped and looked at her mother strangely. They talked no further about it.

Chamis left with Mohammed and told Zahara to finish packing and clean up the place. She should come to Gebulay in a few days to help Chamis in her new home.

The wedding feasting was a quiet affair. Mohammed Abdi's people came to eat and said little. Chamis refused the Midgaan women when she came to open the infibulation. She paid her well so the spirits would smile on her wedding night, but refused to be opened with the knife. "My husband is strong," Chamis boasted. "He will enter me in the true Somali tradition, with his penis." The women ran outside to sing songs taunting the men during the dancing outside.

Chamis thought there must have been an evil spirit in that place, left by the first wife. Mohammed tried to penetrate her all during the night, but he could not. Chamis wondered if there was an evil *jinn* holding her closed. She knew what the women were whispering; "She shouldn't be sleeping in the same bed as Ibado."

Mohammed left in the still darkness before the dawn. Chamis drenched the room with incense to drive away the evil spirit and pulled at her vagina with her own fingers. Why was this going so wrong she wondered.

Early the next day the women came running to tell her about her daughter. Zahara had poured gasoline on her body and lit it. She had not died in the flames but would die soon.

Chamis tore the hair from her head, the skin on her arms, her dress, her face. Physical pain is much easier to bear than the pain of life. The pain in your mind fills up your soul and will not leave you alone. "Beat me," she begged Mohammed. "I must be beaten." He brought her back to Arabsiyo, to Zahara.

Sometimes an entire life is collapsed into a few hours. Zahara's face was not burned, she had poured the gasoline on her dress and when the cotton slip she wore caught fire, no one had been able to pull it off of her body. She never complained about the pain, but she could not be touched. Chamis offered her water, but she would cough and writhe with each spasm, and so she just sat next to her daughter during the long hours of the day. The sun's shadow moved across the floor and out into the desert taking most of Zahara's life with it. If you watched from the doorway, like the other women, you might have thought that nothing happened during that little time of a day. Chamis sat in stillness and silence and watched the hatred gradually fade from her daughter's eyes, then they sat and their eyes met in love and acknowledgment of the unbreakable bond between mother and daughter. In the moonlight, Zahara forgot her argument with life and accepted the will of Allah and the unanswered questions. After the moon set, there was only starlight in her eyes and then it, like hatred and love, gradually faded.

Even though it had been clear from the beginning that Zahara would die during the night, Chamis could not believe it at first, and shook her a little, calling her name. The body was cold.

Chamis screamed and scratched at her face and hair. Mohammed Abdi pulled her away from the body. Worn out by her screaming she saw that Ali Yare had entered the room.

"A man came to the Prophet and wept that his beloved child was dead," Ali Yare said, looking right into her eyes. Chamis couldn't look away from his powerful face. "Mohammed told him to go and dig a well so that others could drink," he told her. Chamis stopped her hysterical thrashing and wept calmly.

Mohammed Abdi and the men buried Zahara that afternoon with the other graves near the gardens. Chamis returned to Gebulay with Mohammed and her duties as a wife. Chamis felt as though her own will had been beaten out of her at every turn and she had been left with the will of Allah. Chamis had no choice but to accept His will and learn to accept the unanswered questions as well. She never passed a grave without putting on another stone, and murmuring a prayer for her daughter, and her mother's daughter, and her grandmother's daughter, and all of the daughters that have been or will be.

The Tree of Life

*The last camel in line
walks as quickly as the first.*

—Somali Proverb

I had been teaching for almost a year yet I was still not confident about my ability to teach. I felt as though I constructed lessons my students would understand without insulting their way of life. However, I only felt that way while I was planning lessons in the security of my house. Whenever I got to class my plans seemed to backfire no matter how carefully I prepared. Even the most innocuous questions often ended up in disaster.

"Who can make up a sentence in English?" I asked my Standard Six class one bright morning.

"A beautiful girl irrigated me yesterday," said Mohammed Abdi, jumping up with a broad smile.

Half the boys laughed, others tried to figure out what my question had been. When Mohammed stood, the scrape of the metal legs of his chair on the cement floor of the classroom destroyed several more nerve endings in my inner ear.

"That remark was very rude," I told him sternly, trying to regain control of the class. I stood as tall as my five feet two inches would allow and told all six feet of him, "Go sit outside the headmaster's office."

"What did I do?" he retorted.

"Mohammed, I'm not taking any more of your lip," I said indignantly, shaking my finger at him for emphasis. I realized, after the words were out of my mouth, that he did not understand "taking any more of your lip." Idiomatic expressions are idiotic when translated literally. Silence descended on the classroom like a power failure. Mohammed, and the rest of Standard Six, stared at me. They were speculating about what the foreign teacher intended to do with his lip.

I was beginning to understand what sour camel's milk had to do with me. I had been nick-named Chino by the villagers. *Chino* is camels' milk that has been buried in the desert for a week in a goat skin. Supposedly, a person becomes intoxicated after drinking it, and I agreed that it probably was toxic. The Quran strictly prohibits Muslims from drinking alcohol but the nomads did make and drink *chino*. I supposed my nickname had to do with the strange behavior the Somalis observed from the American teacher. They found the white woman entertaining, but peculiar.

Well, I thought, I can't possibly explain that I don't really intend to take Mohammed's lip. I pointed to the door and he gathered up his papers. The class remained hushed and frightened as he stalked out of the room. When he reached the door, he turned and gave me a parting look that said: I'd like to see you try taking my lip, lady.

I turned back to my class of forty-eight Somali boys and two girls. Both girls sat together in the front row and threw their veils over their heads whenever I called upon them. Most of the boys sat four to a rickety metal table and two to a chair. This class was a Standard Six and I guessed it was equivalent to a middle school eighth grade class back home. Only talented students would pass the national examination and be able to go on past Standard Eight for further education.

The walls and floor of the classroom were cement. The door opened into a courtyard shared by the other five classrooms that composed Ahmed Gurry Intermediate School. The windows had no glass, only bars and shutters. They sometimes framed the faces of curious nomads and their camels who would stand and watch the class intently for a while. The camels appeared mildly interested, the nomads distrustful. The visitors would sometimes offer a conclusion about their observations, such as "*Sah*" which shows agreement, then move on to the wells outside of town. It amused me that my students, and the camels, often had the same expression of attentive indifference. They both looked as if school was mildly amusing but totally irrelevant.

Somali boys are given one of the ninety-nine names of the Prophet, and the most popular name was Mohammed, or "Servant of God." In fact, most of the boys in my class had Mohammed somewhere in their names. I found this handy when I was calling for order in class. I only had to shout "Mohammed!" and more than half the class would look at me in case I was talking to them.

"Mohammed!" I said, to quell the persistent buzzing that had erupted over Mohammed Abdi's remark and my strange threat to his lip. "Let's return to our English lesson. You must tell me a sentence in English using the past tense. Tell me something that happened to you yesterday."

"Yesterday, I went to the town," offered Ali Abdi shyly.

"Yesterday, I went to the school," continued Ahmed. Each sentence was punctuated by the sharp scrape of the metal chair on the cement floor. I had gotten used to the taste of goat urine and charcoal in my milk, I didn't mind the flies, or the absence of toilet paper, but the screeching of these chairs made me feel like a laboratory rat, endlessly tormented by little electric shocks. Never enough to kill, just enough to slowly make you crazy.

After class I walked over to the headmaster's office for some tea. My fellow teacher, Abdul Kader, was also there. I poured the sweet spicy tea out of the thermos into a short glass, and waited for it to cool enough to drink. Abdul Kader had two glasses and was pouring his tea back and forth between them in the traditional method of cooling tea. The room soon filled with the delicious smell of cinnamon and cloves.

"Why is Mohammed sitting outside?" he asked.

"I sent him out of class for being obnoxious," I replied, sniffing my tea. I could not get enough of the aroma.

"What did he do?"

"He made up a very rude sentence in English."

"What did he say?" Abdul Kader leaned forward in his chair, he was always very interested in knowing what was considered rude in English.

"He said," I replied indignantly, "a beautiful girl irrigated me yesterday." Abdul Kader looked puzzled so I explained. "Irrigated me! It's a sexual statement, don't you think?" I looked at him over my tea glass wondering why he didn't understand.

Instead of commiserating about how difficult the boys could be, Abdul Kader looked bewildered. "I taught that word yesterday in science class," he said after a long pause.

"What did you teach?"

"I gave them a new vocabulary word, irrigate."

"What did you tell them it meant?"

"I dictated a sentence to the class from my science notes," replied Abdul Kader, pointing to his collection of battered notebooks. There were no real books in our school. This little outpost, like most of the others in Somalia, had no money for books. We were very lucky when we had a little paper or chalk. The teachers always complained that the politician's pockets are full of money, the teacher's pockets have only chalk. I would have been happy with some chalk.

The Somali language was not written, because the sheiks could not agree on whether the script should be in Arabic—the holy language of the Quran—or modern

English script. This meant that instruction had to be in English since Somali could not legally be written. Because we had no books, the teachers relied on the notebooks they had copied when they were in school. Whatever material they had copied incorrectly, was faithfully passed on to the new generation of boys lucky enough to be able to go to school. Abdul Kader's notebooks looked as though they had been carried around by an impetuous schoolboy for several years, stuffed in a trunk for a while, and unearthed in desperation when he got a teaching job.

"My definition was, *irrigate: to bring water to*," explained Abdul Kader somberly. "Mohammed was saying, A beautiful girl brought some water to me.' What does that have to do with sex in English?" Abdul Kader was perplexed by what he thought must be a cultural offense.

I stared at the heat rising off the desert outside the window, and the goats climbing up to eat the top leaves on the few scraggly bushes. I didn't know what to say to Abdul Kader, Mohammed, or to myself. I felt foolish, I got angry at all the wrong things and then threatened people's lips. I often missed what was happening entirely, and I had just done it again. Maybe Chino was a good name for me.

I talked to Mohammed who was still sitting in bewilderment outside, and told him that I had made a mistake. I tried to explain that although his sentence was not correct English, I understood that he had not intended to be insulting. My apology did not address the issue of his lip, but I decided it would be better to forget about that part. Mohammed kept his *goa,* or scarf, draped about his neck and mouth during our entire conversation, only his dark glittering eyes showed over the top of it.

We returned to class together and I mentally decided to take over the science classes for the next few weeks. The United States would be putting a man on the moon within the month and I would be able to get some special information about it from the consulate. There was even a chance that I could get a movie to show.

Later that week when I entered the classroom, the cheerful chatter stopped immediately. As they did every morning, the class rose as one and shouted in unison, "Good morning, Sir!"

"Good morning, Standard Six," I replied when I recovered from the shrill rasp of twenty chairs scraping along the floor as my students got up. Then of course, everyone sat back down. Only the steel wheels on the metal tracks of the IRT subway in New York City rivaled the sound of those chairs. I had given up my attempts to explain that I was not "Sir." I had a job, went to the tea shops, rode a horse, and lived away from any members of my family. In the eyes of my students, and the people in town, this was impossible for a woman, therefore I must be a man who looked like a woman. Or maybe, I often mused, I didn't even look like a woman to them. Only Allah knew for sure what sex the white foreigner was.

"Today we will be learning about the solar system." I began. Most of these boys had been awakened by the Mullah's call to the early morning prayers. "*E la he la he ela Allah*, There is no God but Allah." They had taken the family livestock down to the wells for water. Many had climbed into the well and thrown water up to the top in a carved wooden gourd or a water basket. Some of my boys had never seen electric lights, ice, or aerosol. I wondered how these earnest young people could possibly understand jet propulsion. Their sweet, serene faces gazed back at me as I spoke. The soft Arabic features on the mahogany African skin were perfectly proportioned. I had never seen such uniformly beautiful people, or such bored students.

"The Americans have built a rocket and are sending it all the way through the sky to the moon. . . . " No response. "It will have to have three parts because the moon is so far away." Vague disbelief, not about the rocket but the distance to the moon. "One of the stages will hold the astronauts. The other two will fall off when all of the petrol they carry has been used," I said. I couldn't tell if my class didn't understand the English words, what I was talking about, or both.

"It is a long way to the moon." I tried making the idea easier in a bid for comprehension. Blank faces gazed up at me. Sounds of the wooden bells on the camels being irrigated at the wells wafted gently through the room. It gave me a nice dose of reality.

I had expected more of a reaction to the news of a rocket going to the moon, but the class had an "and then what" attitude. They had observed many incomprehensible pieces of technology and they had little idea what was new and what was old. Land Rovers, trucks, and airplanes had rolled across the desert before many people in the nomadic clans had seen a key open a lock. They had not been part of the gradual development of technology in the rest of the world, now they were having sophisticated products dropped into their midst.

Everybody had heard the radio because all of the tea shops had one. Radio Hargeisa had been established for several years and was broadcasting twelve hours a day in Somali throughout the Northern region. However, there were still those people who answered the voices on the radio as if a person were actually sitting inside the little black box and required acknowledgment.

After explaining the industrial revolution in the West to my class, I had posed the question, "Has there been an industrial revolution in Somalia?" My students were almost evenly divided between those who felt that Somalia had been industrialized, and those who did not. I carefully refrained from taking sides.

Yesterday a woman had begged me to fix the shattered glass lining of her thermos bottle. She waited patiently outside the school office until after classes. When I came out she pleaded with me to repair it. The hapless woman cried that her husband would beat her if he found out it was broken. She simply would not accept that I could not fix broken glass. I felt so badly that I gave her some money for a new thermos. Abdillahi, my headmaster, laughed at me and shouted at her to get out of the schoolyard.

"She deserves to be beaten." he said. "If she really thinks that you have the power to mend broken glass because you are an American, she is stupid."

"What is so bad about giving her a little money?" I asked, feeling defensive.

" Jeanne," he replied, "when you give her money to fix the thermos because she thought Americans can fix glass, you act like you are some sort of God. You perpetuate her belief that you can fix everything." He was right, I supposed. It did give her the wrong idea, and it did make me feel powerful. The interface between the world I came from, and the Somali way of life, was difficult and hard to sort out. Everyone had an agenda about development, and was mainly interested in protecting their own interests. I was no exception.

The Somalis were quite used to seeing satellites. They knew they were sent into the sky by the Russians and the Americans. My students were casually accepting of a manned rocket going to the moon. If you could send someone from Hargeisa to talk in a little box, why couldn't you send someone to the moon? The class listened patiently to my lecture, and watched with blank faces the drawings and pictures I showed to illustrate my points.

I finished my science lesson with the topic for the following day, "The rocket will land on the moon's surface and the astronauts will get out and walk on the moon." This last statement finally caused a whisper of surprise to race around the classroom. If men would get out and step on the moon, this was different from the radio where the people were never actually seen. At last my students were intrigued I thought, little suspecting what the excited whispers were all about, and the trouble that lay ahead.

That night, two of my students, Mohammed Attah and Ali Abdi, came to my house on the outskirts of town to visit. When the moon was full it illuminated the rocky paths and everyone went out to make calls on their friends. When the moon was new, everyone stayed home and slept early. That night the moon was divided precisely in half as if it had been dipped in chocolate.

"Come in boys, come in boys," I gestured, holding open the thin wooden door with no lock or key, only a bolt to hold it shut.

Tall and lanky, the boys had easily walked through the town unperturbed by the wild dogs or hyenas that roamed the streets after dark. Now they crouched behind one another in the doorway, frightened by my kitty cat. "She won't hurt you, it's just my kitty, " I said, taking her up into my arms. However, neither boy would enter the house as long as she was in the room, and I locked her spoiled highness in the courtyard. They wore the white shirts and khaki shorts that were the uniform of the schoolboy. Mohammed was so tall and angular that his long legs looked like tent poles. He had an endearing face and a sad droop to his eyes. I always wanted to hug him. Ali Abdi was one of the most intelligent young boys I had ever met. He spoke Somali, Arabic, French, and English.

"Miss Jeanne," began Ali Abdi, "my family is very upset about the rocket."

"What is it about the rocket that is a problem, Ali?" I asked.

"My uncle is afraid the rocket will kill all the Somalis."

"Ali, it won't go near Somalia. Why would the Americans want to kill the Somalis?"

"But, Miss Jeanne," he continued, "it says in the Quran that there is a tree on the moon. When a Somali is born, a new leaf grows on the tree. When your leaf falls from the tree, you will die."

"If the Americans land on the moon, the rocket may come down on the tree, or disturb it in some way and all the Somalis will die before it is their time," added Mohammed.

"Boys," I reassured them, "there is no air or water on the moon. A tree can't grow on the moon. Tomorrow in school I will show you some pictures of the moon's surface. It shows that the moon is actually a barren desert where nothing can survive." I talked very slowly, seeing the distrust in their eyes that did not abate. They were distinctly not convinced and I realized, in the silence that followed, that the Somalis had survived for centuries on a barren desert and there were trees there as well. Actually the pictures of the moon did look a little bit like the area surrounding our little town. When you get to know the desert, it is full of color and design, but you must learn to look closely. A casual glance by those not familiar with its secrets does not reveal what is hidden by the glare of the sun.

Ali Abdi and Mohammed stared at me. They were trying to translate my English into Somali words and then into what they knew of the world outside my door. Despite our conversation, I could tell that they were still skeptical when they left. They started to argue in heated Somali as soon as I said goodnight but they did not waken my sleeping watchman, Osman Tuuk. He continued to snore loudly in the little shack he had constructed outside my door.

The boys followed the rocky path from my house back into the village, a short distance away. Their two shapes cast long shadows, but the moon did not follow them. She waited right above my head. The light of the moon, a borrowed light, gave an illusory appearance to everything, and I fretted about shapes I saw in the distance. The boys knew every rock in the village, they were not easily frightened by anything native to Somalia. They were however, disturbed by news from the Western world that called into question some very ancient traditions. The villagers struggled with the way I lived and many of the things I talked about. My presence there threatened old beliefs and the comforting, familiar world of the village. Now Chino was challenging a religious presumption.

The half moon was setting in the night sky, and I looked to see if I could find one of the traveling satellites called *hydigi 'mericans*, or American stars, by the local people. I decided to be very careful in my classes about what I said about the lunar landing. It is written that when you have found the beginning of the way, the stars will guide you. I watched to see what the stars had to tell me because I was beginning to fear that I had gotten into something ominous with my moon walk lessons.

The next day, armed with pictures from the American Consulate in Hargeisa, I continued to discuss the plans for the lunar landing. The class was unusually attentive and most of the things I said were immediately translated into Somali by the better students. Comments buzzed quickly through the room. "There is no oxygen on the moon so nothing can live there," I stated to youngsters who had never heard of oxygen and were very suspicious about what a teacher said who was not Muslim and threatened people's lips.

I tried a more practical approach. "The rocket is like the airplanes that land at the airstrip in Hargeisa." (Whenever there are no goats on the runway, I thought wryly to myself.) Even if the boys had not seen the airplanes they had at least heard of them, or there were enough boys who had, to convince the rest of the class that this indeed was true. "The rocket will take off in a vertical position rather than horizontally, but it is the same idea as the airplanes." Hearing a loud "*Sah*" from the class, I thought—rather unwisely—success at last.

Over the following weeks I gave up trying to discredit the notion of a tree on the moon. I was calling into question the very Quran and risked insulting my student's religion. I stopped bringing up this strange notion of scientific proof and the inability of trees to grow on the moon. In my own country, most people accepted the virgin birth of Jesus, despite its scientific improbability. We didn't discuss this issue in science classes stateside, and I decided it would be the better part of valor not to dispute the Somali notion of "The Tree of Life." The Somalis revere Jesus, the son of Mary, as a prophet, not a God. They question the reality of his virgin birth and resurrection from the dead. The *Shahada*, "There is no God, but God," is recited every time Muslims gather to pray and is the profession of faith upon which the rest of the pillars of Islam are based. My students had a hard time understanding how Christians profess to worship one God, yet believe in a Father, Son, and Holy Spirit. They would often ask why I had three Gods, but pretended to worship one. I could not explain the resurrection and I decided not to dispute the presence of a tree on the moon. Obviously, neither religion had anything over the other in the scientific fact department.

I did attempt to reassure my classes that the rocket would not come near the alleged tree. "The rocket is small and the moon is big," I said. "It will not land on the tree." However, I could see that half the boys had seen the aircraft that flew into Somalia, and obviously everyone watched the moon and knew what size that was. In the eyes of my students, long disciplined to be acutely aware of their surroundings, the rocket seemed awfully big compared to the tiny moon they saw in the night sky. My assurances that the rocket would miss the moon tree were not very logical or reassuring.

The American consulate was doing an incredible job of getting teaching materials to my post. I had no books at the school, and we ran out of paper during the first week, but I got posters and pictures of the rocket and the lunar landscape almost every week when the truck came in from Hargeisa. Then came the big news. The consulate would be getting films about the moon shot and perhaps even actual pictures of the landing. They would send a Land Rover with a movie projector and generator out to the village. We could show the movies of the moon walk on the whitewashed wall in the school yard. It was probable that this would happen the night after the lunar landing. I was stunned. Letters often took a month or more from home, but I would get a movie from the moon the very next day. Even I was very excited about the technology involved in this operation.

"Everyone is invited to see the movies," I told my classes. "You can bring your fathers and mothers and all of the elders who have been talking with you about this. They will be able to see that what you are learning about in school is actually true." I wanted to help my students convince the village elders that school was not a waste of time. Hopefully they would see that I was not teaching their children foolish ideas in opposition to the traditional knowledge of the Somali clans.

On the night of the actual lunar landing, the moon over Arabsiyo was full and rose bright saffron yellow over the village. Everyone watched the moon for signs of the American rocket. I had spent my final classes explaining that the rocket would be too small and far away to see, but I too, sat outside my house and watched for signs of it. I was caught up in anticipation like my students and, like everyone else, I was disappointed. The moon did not reveal her secrets to those who waited in the little village of Arabsiyo.

I knew that my friends back home in Ann Arbor were

also watching, as were people in Moscow, Hang Chow, Cusco, and Kathmandu. I felt as though the world had stopped to hold its breath and was, for once in its entire history, united with a single purpose. Together, the world's people marveled at the face of the moon and the courage of men and women. I felt very peaceful in the stillness of the sleeping desert that night. The moon however, like the camels framed in my classroom window, was impassive. She sat in the sky as she always had, shining down on my village with the contentment of one who knows that all is one. It is only human beings who try so hard to find the differences between people, tribes, nations, and stars.

The following night, like the preceding, featured the sunset, then a gallery of stars. This was followed by the main attraction, the full golden moon gracefully rising over the desert. It called the entire population of Arabsiyo to the school yard for the social event of the year. As promised, a Land Rover fitted with a gas generator had arrived with, not one, but two, films of the moon shot. One was actual footage of Neil Armstrong stepping down onto the moon. The other was an animated documentary explaining the three stage rocket, technical assistance teams, weightlessness in space, and space suits. It had pictures of a simulated moon walk in a studio. I decided to show the actual footage of the moon walk first. Later I wondered if that was my mistake.

An enthusiastic crowd of about 100 people had already gathered in the school yard when I arrived with the Somali driver, Ali Esa, and the Land Rover. Mohammed Attah and Ali Abdi pushed their way through the crowd and greeted me. "Everyone is very excited," they told me. "One of the sheiks is here to see this moon movie."

Ali Esa backed the Land Rover into the courtyard after Ali Abdi chased the little kids, to get them out of the way so we could get the car into position. More people had arrived and it was difficult to maneuver the jeep. Ali Esa was hesitant to bring the car into the back of the courtyard. "Some of these people are angry," he said. Ali Esa was usually so calm and placid it alarmed me that he was worried.

"After they see the movie, and that the rocket did not

come anywhere near the Somali tree, they will understand," I assured him confidently.

As we set up the movie projector, people sat on the ground in the courtyard. I saw many of my students and waved cheerfully at them. They did not wave back, but waited nervously in little groups. Only Mohammed and Ali Abdi stood with us on the open back of the Land Rover. I thought the crowd was impatient and expected things to settle down and the mood to soften when the movie finally started to roll. The film was actual footage of the moon walk, and it had been broadcast on television sets all over the world. The picture was grainy and flickered as you would expect from something broadcast back to Earth from the moon.

It was not well received by the fitful crowd. Several rocks were thrown at the screen and persistent undertones grew louder and louder. People began to shout and I turned to Mohammed for a translation. I could not understand the rapid Somali or the growing animosity of the crowd. It was still getting larger as more people entered the school yard.

"The people are saying that this movie is a fake," Mohammed told me. "They say the Americans are trying to trick the Somalis into believing they went to the moon. "Miss Jeanne," he questioned me directly, "nobody saw any rockets last night. If we can see the satellites why didn't anybody see the rockets?"

Well, I knew the picture was grainy and flickered in black and white. It looked like those early television shows of The Lone Ranger. Of course none of the people in my village had seen early television or Tonto. The picture wasn't good visually and they thought it was a fake. It was a short film however, and we quickly put on the next tape of the documentary.

This film was in color and the photographs were clear. The crowd settled down to watch. I was relieved. I didn't want the families of my students to go home convinced that I was teaching them lies in school. They sacrificed the labor of the boys to send them to school. They could easily pull all my pupils and take them back to tend the camel herds in the interior.

Attentive silence filled the courtyard during the second film. Some of my students could follow the dialogue and were translating for their families. The movie was well done, and despite the language barrier, the ideas were graphically expressed with models and props. The three stage propulsion rocket was demonstrated with a little model. The command centers were shown, and space suits were demonstrated. Shots of the weightless astronauts floating around the cabin drew gasps from the audience. At last I thought, they believe it! Unfortunately it was true, the villagers had begun to believe that the American rocket had landed on the surface of the moon.

The mood tensed and gradually escalated into hostility when the simulation of the moon walk began. The exterior of the rocket showed on the corner of the screen and the camera panned the set of the lunar moonscape. A rock hit the wall of the school in the middle of the picture. When the door of the rocket slid open, more rocks were thrown. When the actor in the space suit ventured down the ladder to step onto the ancient dust covering the moon, the school yard erupted. Suddenly the screen was pelted with rocks, then many people turned to the Land Rover. Angry men climbed on the wheels of the jeep to scream in my face.

"American!"

"New York!"

"Kennedy." These were the only English words most people knew and they shouted them in my face. Immense anger was apparent, no matter what the actual words used to express it were. I was stunned for a moment. I couldn't wrap my mind around what was happening. Foolishly I tried to explain.

"Wait a minute," was all I got out before a rock hit me in the back, and another followed. More rocks missed me but hit Mohammed and Ali Abdi who were in front of me. Someone reached up to grab me off the back of the Land Rover and Mohammed pulled me into the open back of the jeep. Ali Esa was shouting that if people didn't sit back down he would stop the movie, but no one heard. Women were screaming, babies were crying, children began to run around in the confusion. Rocks continued to hit the projector, Ali Abdi, Mohammed and me.

"Get inside quickly, sir," said Ali Abdi, pushing and pulling me toward the front of the jeep. He was quite frightened, and that alarmed me more than the shouting. He forced the door of the cab open by hitting several women in front of it with a stick, and I climbed in. Ali Esa was already in the driver's seat and he locked the door seconds before hands grabbed the handle.

"Let's get out of here," he said. "These people are nuts." He started the jeep and we just left the projector still rolling in the back. He turned on the car lights and honked the horn surprising everyone, he rammed the Land Rover into first gear. Mohammed and Ali Abdi jumped into the back with the movie projector and turned it over so it would not fall out. This ended any semblance of order and the crowd surged around the vehicle, shrieking and hurling stones.

"Get down" called Ali Esa, as a rock bounced off the rear window and shattered it into a thousand pieces, all over the boys in the back. I was crying on the floor and shaking because I was so mad and so confused. What was the matter with these people? I felt the truck lurch ahead and stop short over and over. Miraculously no one was injured that I know of, and we made our way out of the courtyard and through the empty streets of the town.

Ali Esa decided he had had quite enough of Arabsiyo and dropped me off at home with Mohammed and Ali Abdi. He went back to Hargeisa and the safety of the American Consulate garage that night, using the bright light of the still dispassionate moon to guide him on the darkened track which leads through the desert.

I bolted my door firmly against this bizarre night. Osman Tuuk, the worthless watchman, was watching elsewhere the one time I needed him. Mohammed and Ali Abdi, who had been unafraid of the mob of villagers, cowered when kitty pranced into the room. I'll never understand Somalis, I thought, putting my baby kitty firmly out into the courtyard.

I lit my oil lamps, one after the other against the darkness of this frightening evening. The lamps have a soft light which is comforting when things are quiet, but at the time I really wanted a searing searchlight to see what was going on. Fortunately I suppose, I didn't have a giant light to draw any more attention to myself or the twentieth century than I already had.

Ali Abdi and Mohammed were philosophical. "The people think you were insulting them with the first movie," said Mohammed, and Ali Abdi agreed. "They thought it was a fake made up by the Americans to fool the Somalis. You could tell it was just a fake by the way it looked."

"Well, that's show biz," I said to blank looks.

"Then, when they saw the second movie, the people became very upset. That movie was real and then everyone believed in the moon walk. The people don't feel that the Americans had a right to go to the moon," explained Ali Abdi carefully. "It is the sacred place of the holy tree to the Somalis. Why do the Americans think they can just go and take over the moon?"

Mohammed added, "Everyone was shouting that the moon belongs to the Somalis."

"Besides that," continued Ali Abdi, "everyone was frightened about the tree. They couldn't see it when the picture showed the moon. My uncle thought maybe the rocket landed on the tree."

"Nobody has died so most people think the rocket missed the Somali tree," said Mohammed.

"Will you get in trouble with your families for being with me tonight?" I asked.

"I am always in trouble about the school, about English, about Americans," replied Mohammed with a little laugh. I think that he enjoyed harassing his elders, like most adolescents. Like most Somalis he was fiercely independent. One does not survive in this harsh climate without thinking for oneself. There are no kings in Somalia. Each person is equal to every other person.

Responsibility for oneself is nurtured by the culture and respected. My young students were growing into Somali men. The tradition of unbridled self-reliance engendered by desert water rights would be carried on to issues raised by modern technology. I wondered how they would handle the growing barrage of Western influences. I didn't know how old beliefs could be carried forward without a civil war between the modern and the traditional. I feared that this little undeveloped country was becoming so stressed by the technology invading its borders that it would result in tragedy. I especially worried what modern weaponry would do when dropped into a country with no infrastructure strong enough to hold back the bullets. In the traditional Somali culture physical blows settled differences, then compensation was paid to the wounded party. What would happen if Somali men got machine guns and used them to decide disputes instead of throwing rocks? When some individuals rejected the tribal system and refused to pay compensation? I shuddered to think what could happen. I was glad the country was too poor to equip an army and hoped no nation would ever give them modern weaponry.

"Do you think there will be trouble in town or at school about this?" I asked.

"Everyone will talk and talk about this for weeks," said Mohammed. "Everybody in town will have a different opinion."

"Most people are glad that you brought the movies," said Ali Abdi. "They don't hate you for telling us what is happening in the rest of the world."

"I think a lot of these people in town are stupid, " said Mohammed, his head in his hands. "The Americans are going to the moon and the Somali people don't even know how to make a needle."

Ali Abdi, however, was defiant about the incident and I loved him for his pride and the lesson he taught me. "We have a Somali proverb," he said, sitting with beautiful posture as always, erect with quiet grace and dignity. "The last camel in line walks as quickly as the first." The last country in the world is affected by the leading nations. This is one planet, what happens to the least of us, happens to the rest of us.

Tea for Two More

Women are the devil's snares.
—Somali Proverb

The wonders of civilization I thought, as I sat in the lobby of the Shebelli hotel. It was a reasonable hotel by Somali standards. There were four floors of passably clean rooms and functional furnishings. The water in the bathrooms was sea water, but it was a treat to me. I liked to turn on the faucet just to watch it run. I had been living in tiny Arabsiyo in the middle of the desert for over a year and was enthralled by anything liquid that came out of pipes. I was in Mogadishu to work on a special project to train the new Peace Corps volunteers and I took full advantage of any convenience.

In the hotel lobby, I watched a determined middle-aged Somali man dressed in khaki pants and a white shirt struggle to get his aged father up to a room in the hotel.

They had already tried the elevator. The old man, obviously fresh from the bush, was totally unacquainted with the notion of buildings with a second floor, electricity, pulleys, or glass. He was dressed in a *ma'aweiss* and had a long white beard underneath small black eyes gleaming with anger. The fierce old nomad had watched the elevator doors open and close with grave composure while leaning on his gnarled walking stick. He observed the people getting into the little box, and then he saw that they disappeared. He found the fact that they had been taken up in the air rather alarming. His son had almost managed to get him inside the elevator, but when the doors started to close, the old man panicked and began to beat at everything with his stick, flailing his son and several other passengers. "This is an insult to the Prophet and to Allah!" he shouted.

Father and son squatted on the floor beside the vexatious elevator. They had a long, punctuated discussion concerning the fact that elevators were not mentioned in the Quran.

"Father, times have changed since the Prophet lived."

"The Quran is timeless."

"Mohammed would have gone on elevators, but they are run by electricity, and there was no electricity when he lived."

"Then where did electricity come from?"

"It's the same thing as lightning but in wires." This explanation was met with such a look at the doors where people disappeared by lightning, that the son sighed and gave up. "Let's try the stairs again, *Aba*," he pleaded. "It's like climbing up the side of a riverbank, that's all." It was hard for me to tell when a person was exasperated when the conversation was in Somali, but this sounded like it.

They ventured over to the staircase in the middle of the lobby. The son had supportive assistance from two of the hotel patrons, but his father remained reluctant. The desk clerk followed the proceedings with rapt attention despite the growing line in front of his desk. No one complained about waiting and I assumed they were sympathetic. This could have been any one of the modern Somali men waiting to check into the hotel. They might have encountered similar difficulties trying to deal with a relative from the bush visiting the big city of Mogadishu.

With a concentrated effort, the little group put the unwilling nomad's feet on the first step, but Aba leaned further backward in a misguided effort to stay perpendicular. He insisted on putting his feet on the wrong surface of the step. Ultimately he had to be carried up the stairs by the three men, because he tenaciously placed both feet squarely on the vertical back of each step. I hoped his son had booked a room on the first floor. I wondered what had become of the elderly man's natural sense of himself in space, and finally decided he was just being stubborn. I suspect he was proving to his son that the city was unnatural and that the open desert was the only place for devout Muslims to live.

Aba must have mastered either the stairs or the elevator, because I saw him outside the hotel the next day. He was leaning on his walking stick looking quite dignified with the crowd of people who gathered to watch the washing machines. There were three machines, with glass doors, conveniently placed so they faced the street, in the window of the Chinese laundry. It could have been televisions that were displayed, given the rapt attention and the animated discussions which took place among the watchers. Sometimes I stopped to admire the show myself. The whirling mixture of soap, water, and colorful clothing was highlighted by surprise starts and stops, each accented by different speeds. The final spin, when everything was compacted into the sides of the machine, was always a dramatic finale. It seemed as though the whirling motion would get out of control and throw everything out, but it never did. With a terrific purr, like a pleased lion, the machine wound down to a stop, sans water, sans soap, sans the bulky cloth present during the performance. When the attendant came to remove the flattened load, most people nodded to show their appreciation of "Somali television" and the laundryman bowed.

After watching the soaps for a while, I stopped by the

Russian dairy to buy some milk. I had heard that they had ice cold pasteurized milk and I was very anxious to try it. Sure enough, inside the refrigerated dairy cases were neat rows of shining glass bottles.

In a country where milk is one of the staple foods, it was hard for me to drink it. The nomads had little water in the desert, so they carefully cleaned out the carved wooden milk *dhills* with goat urine. Then they sterilized the inside with hot coals from the cooking fires. This left a residue which made the milk taste like it had been charcoal broiled. I like charcoal flavor on steak, not in milk. The milk also had a faint musky tang but I tried not to think about that.

I bought some milk in the immaculate dairy and eagerly opened the icy bottle to drink the pure white contents. However, I almost choked on the chilled drink. The Russians had put charcoal in the milk! My friends explained that the Somalis had refused to buy the plain milk, claiming it tasted suspicious. The Russians had given in to local convention and added charcoal flavoring to their milk. After tasting it, I decided I preferred authentic goat urine and ashes to artificial charcoal. Who knew what was in that fake flavoring, it might be a communist plot.

That night, I had been invited to attend a dinner party at the American ambassador's residence to welcome the new consul for the North. He was on his way to Hargeisa, the capital city of the North, where he and his wife would run the consulate. Since receiving the embossed white invitation, I thought constantly about the dinner because real American food would be served. I was very excited about my first dinner party in an actual embassy with a *bona fide* ambassador serving edible food. I had seen the official residence from the street, massive and gleaming white, with a uniformed guard standing at a wrought iron fence. As an ordinary American in the States, my opportunities to attend social functions on embassy row were non-existent. However, as one of the few Americans living in Somalia, my social status had dramatically improved. I was invited to attend an actual diplomatic function at a live embassy. I had dreamed for weeks of white gloved servants taking my coat, passing out hors d'oeuvres, pouring drinks, serving dinner, pouring wine, serving seconds, pouring coffee, serving dessert, serving seconds, offering liquors, and passing out little mints. I thought about smooth elegant silver, china plates, and crystal goblets gleaming on a snow white tablecloth. I had endured a steady diet of rice served on a tin plate, with a cup of grey milk, in a house with a tin roof, a jug for water, army ants, and a dirt floor. I couldn't wait to tread on a carpet, to sit on a toilet seat, and perhaps, oh wonder of wonders, to see my reflection in a full sized mirror. My little pocket mirror was the only one in Arabsiyo.

That night, my expectations were met. The carpet was soft, the scotch was good, there was plenty of food, and I had lost so much weight in Arabsiyo that I stuffed myself with impunity. However, I found sitting on the toilet seat uncomfortable after squatting over the hole on the long drop for so many months. When I turned on the faucet it spattered everything including my dress. The full length mirror reflected a woman badly in need of a haircut.

The dinner was exceptional and more than made up for any misfortunes. Each dish was brought out on a silver tray covered with an equally silver top to keep it hot. Mashed potatoes, meat and gravy, and actual green beans were served. Each portion was carefully placed on my plate by a white gloved servant using two spoons and one hand. I was more than impressed, I was in diplomatic heaven. After everyone was served, we waited for the ambassador, a single father, to begin. I looked down the row of twenty guests to the head of the table. Ambassador MacDonald's seven-year-old son had refused all of the food offered by the parade of servants. He sat with an empty plate and a frowning father. Suddenly, the kitchen doors opened and yet another covered silver tray flashed by. It held a bowl which was served with a flourish to the boy. "He only eats corn flakes," explained his father dryly, lifting his fork so his guests could begin to eat.

I had seen a little metal screw, perhaps from the lid of a cooking pot, mixed with the green beans that had been placed on my plate by the white gloved waiter. Feeling so elegant, I did not want anything to mar the magnificence of the lovely dinner. I surreptitiously fished the screw out of the beans and hid it in my pocket. I intended to give it to one of the servants after the meal so as not to embarrass the ambassador. My little secret was revealed however, by the chef who burst out of the kitchen in the middle of the meal, followed by one of the waiters without his white gloves. They stood for a moment looking at the table full of surprised diners, then the waiter pointed a bony finger right at me.

"Give it to me," demanded the chef, after he had checked the food remaining on my plate and the table around it. Everyone sitting at the diner table looked at me in amazement. "I know that you took it," the chef said accusingly.

I knew exactly what he was referring to, and so there was nothing to do but reach into my pocket and withdraw the little screw. The chef marched triumphantly back into the kitchen holding his conquest high in the air, followed by the self-righteous waiter. Everyone at the dinner very politely treated the incident as if it never happened, but I noticed several people checking around in the food on their plates for additional treasures.

"I understand that you have many female friends in the North," said Jack, the new consul, during coffee in the library after dinner. He was well rounded and fair, about fifty years old and he had an amiable manner. I liked him, but then I hadn't seen anyone in a suit and tie in over twelve months.

"I have met some wonderful women," I said. "I have a lot in common with the Somali women who have studied abroad. We are both definite curiosities to the local people who are often threatened by the ideas we bring up. The women I know are trying to balance traditional ways of life with the twentieth century."

"My wife is very interested in women's issues," he replied, "especially what women are facing in Muslim countries."

"There are certainly a lot of difficult issues here for

women. Most of the innovations for women began with prostitutes." His eyes lit up with interest, and I wondered how long his wife had been away. "Proper Somali women veiled themselves in *purdah* until the prostitutes started walking around town in their colorful dresses. Eventually all the women dropped the black robes. The prostitutes were the first to send their daughters to school, in an effort to give their female children an alternative to prostitution. Now there are other girls who are being educated and the number is growing."

"Would you be willing to introduce my wife, Susan, to some of the important women in the North? She will be arriving next week."

"It would be a real pleasure," I said, surprised that he would trust his wife to a known thief. "I could invite the women to a sundowner, it's like a cocktail party but without the alcohol since no one here drinks. Since it will be all women, it will be more like a tea party." He agreed, and we settled on a date soon after she would arrive. I was left to worry about what kind of food I could find given the limited options available in Arabsiyo, and my distinct lack of silver, china, white gloves, or toilet seats. I did have a servant, Osman the Thief, my night watchman, but I didn't think putting Osman in gloves would help.

I invited Asha, whose father had been a diplomat in London. She had been raised there, and she spoke fluent English, Arabic, and Somali. I also asked Halimo and Amina. Asha had introduced me to them. They were both nurses at the Hargeisa hospital. They had studied nursing in London together. When I met her, Halimo had just returned from her nursing studies in England. At first the British had called her "that dirty African," but as she learned to emulate the ways of the English they began to consider her delightful and beautiful. Halimo also found the habits of the British very confounding. She described how a person would be in the middle of something or just about to start, or even just about to finish. Rather than continue with what was happening, they would suddenly leave and go to have a cup of tea. Halimo could never figure out why they just got up and left. I couldn't imagine this myself, until I finally determined that it was "break" time. When she learned to stop trying to complete the job at hand and to join the others at "tea," they stopped considering her "dirty."

Both Halimo and her partner at the hospital, Amina Nur, were very interested in meeting someone who cared about the special difficulties encountered by Muslim women. I also invited Muslima, who was a was a teacher at the girl's school on the other side of town. She and I had decided to start a girl scout troop for the girls in our schools. I invited the District Commissioner's wife, Ibado. She had been raised in Aden, travelled frequently to Saudi Arabia, and had recently returned from a visit abroad. I invited Assia, she was married to Hajji Mohammed who worked at the consulate. There would be six women altogether. Intelligent, of course tall, and of course, beautiful. They were life preservers for me as I tried to understand why people threw rocks at the car whenever I drove or threw rocks at me when, walking to school, I took a short cut through the *aquals* outside of town. They also knew what to do with the weevils in the flour.

"Well, they don't hurt you," said Asha when I fretted about what the American woman would think about the weevils. I worried despite her reassurances. It was impossible to buy any flour that was not crawling with little white worms. There were no pastry shops or bakeries in town and I would have to prepare everything myself. "The heat in the baking kills them and they are actually protein," Asha said to console me. It was great having a friend who had both attended college in London and was knowledgeable about nomadic ways, but did she have to be so optimistic?

"But they look so horrible."

"Sift them out then."

"Asha," I complained, "they leave such a terrible flavor in the flour. Everything I bake tastes like weevil to me."

"Use heavy seasoning to disguise the taste," she answered. Asha was always so resourceful. She had to be, given what little food or other supplies were available on a regular basis in Somalia. "How about chocolate? You can get that in town. You won't taste the weevils over the chocolate flavor."

And so I decided to make a chocolate cake and chocolate cookies. I sent Osman Tuuk, my night watchman, to buy a new charcoal stove so I would have two stoves for the baking. "Seven shillings for this?" I complained when he brought it, even though I knew it would not do any good. "Osman, these cost five shillings in the market."

"Mistress, this stove is very strong, it will bake everything perfectly," he said in his innocently booming voice.

"Osman, if I didn't need this I'd make you take it back." I gave him the seven shillings and we were both satisfied with the deal. He cheated on the price, I complained enough to keep the stealing down to a minimum. It was a mutually satisfactory arrangement. Wits count for as much as money in a Somali transaction. I was grateful Osman had brought the stove when I needed it, not a week later, which usually seemed to happen. I didn't mind the extra shillings but felt I had to complain to maintain decent standards of extortion.

The stoves were made of recycled ten-gallon oil tins. The top of the square container was cut off with tin snips, and an eight inch square opening was cut into one side. The tin from the top and side were cut into strips and used to make a lattice. This was fitted inside the top of the stove, about three inches from the upper lip. The charcoal was placed on the lattice and the ashes from the fire dropped down into the bottom. Air circulated to keep the coals burning through the square cut into the side.

I bought a large pot with a flat lid in the market to use as an oven. I placed the double chocolate cake in a round pan inside the big pot and carefully placed it on the hot coals. I put more glowing coals on top of the flat lid. This created an "oven." I gave Osman the newspaper cone the flour had come in and told him to use it to fan the coals. He obediently squatted in front of the stove and fanned frantically for thirty minutes to keep the oven at 350 degrees. He was pretty good at fanning, I thought, and it seemed to keep him awake. Finally I had a good use for this wretched man, whom Abdillahi, my headmaster, had insisted I hire as a night watchman. I had decided to make the best of it, but I often found myself sighing about the will of Allah.

My cat, Malvey, watched from the corner. She didn't like the stoves, but she was interested in the smells which filled up the cool night air. She had seven distinct black rings around her tail and I thought she was half domestic and half ring-tailed wild cat. I had picked her up from a hole behind the little open air market place in town and brought the poor starving animal back home with me. She was skinny and crying so pitifully for something to eat that it broke my heart and my resistance. I knew that if the Somalis found her, they would stone her to death. They don't like cats, and I imagined that was what happened to her mother and the rest of the litter. At first I thought she was grey. She was crawling with fleas and the first thing I did when I got her home was to give her a bath. She was too weak and little to complain about it. The water turned black and she turned white, except for the rings on her tail, much to my surprise. White with black specs, however. The black specs turned out to be hideous fleas, stunned by the water and clinging to her wet fur. I picked them off one by one, and squeezed them between my fingers to kill the bastards. After kitty was clean and drying in the afternoon sun that lingered in my courtyard, I went to sweep up the little pile of fleas and throw them into the long drop once and for all. Much to my dismay they had recovered from the water and were gone! I saw the last one crawl into the mat before I could grab it. Osman had watched this with a look of total disgust on his face, and I had to tell him in no uncertain terms that he needed to guard the kitty as well as me.

Malvey had her definite likes and dislikes. She liked playing with insects when she could find them, she liked to sleep next to the water jug . She did not like Osman, who hated her right back. It was poetic justice, I had to put up with him sleeping when he was supposed to be guarding the house, and he had to put up with her clawing at his legs. Just another happy family I thought to myself, watching him watching her watching him fan the cake.

Each day I scoured the market and the shops in hopes of finding that new food shipments had arrived from somewhere. I decided against serving the tins of Chinese tuna fish which always gave me diarrhea. I ate it anyway with cans of beans when I was really hungry. It was a simple case of eat now, pay later. I also refused to serve any of the ancient Chinese canned pineapple. Every store in every town had stacks of cans they had purchased years ago. They were served as a special treat for the foreigner whenever I visited anyone's home, and I was so sick of it I didn't want to look at it. Whoever that Chinese salesman was, he or she was incredible. I figured there was enough pineapple in town to last several more years given the current rate of foreign visitations.

As luck would have it, I did find tins of cheese in Ali Yare's store one afternoon. Thrilled, not only for the party, but for myself, I bought most of the cans he had. What a treasure I thought carrying them home. They were tins of yellow cheese and were clearly American. Each can was marked, "Gift of the American People: Not to be Sold." They had been pilfered from the U.S. food aide shipments. They had been sold to merchants who sold them back to the Americans because the Somalis don't eat cheese. I was thrilled to have this gift from the American people to serve to the consul's wife. Ah! The wonders of graft, I thought, as I happily skipped home carrying this marvelous edible treasure.

The day of the sundowner was beautiful as usual. My house was clean, and I even swept the endless dust that blows in from the desert off of my front steps. Only Osman's grubby little sleeping box in the front looked disgusting. He refused to take it down, saying he would be attacked by wild hyenas if he just guarded the house by sitting up outside. I had given up trying to convince him he was supposed to stay awake if he was a night watchman.

My cat had been up most of the night, pacing frantically back and forth. I had finally opened the bedroom door and let her into the courtyard so I could get some sleep. She had whimpered for some time out there. She is afraid, I thought in my sleep. I had wild dreams of all sorts of animals crawling over the sides of the house and crying to be fed.

I was awakened by a yowl that started at the base of my spine and ran up my back like falling into an icy lake. I sat bolt upright in bed trying to figure out who had attacked my usually peaceful abode. I finally realized it was Malvey who was racing about the courtyard howling and shrieking. She would not let me touch her, and just kept darting back and forth in front of the outside wall of the courtyard. She had come into heat. This was not domestic cat heat, kitty was in wildcat heat. My cuddly little kitty cat was gone, this new cat was possessed by surging passion, she was unrestrained by the bonds of civility, friendship, loyalty, or gratitude. Malvey looked as though she was perfectly willing to kill me, or anyone else who was foolish enough to stand in her way, to get what she wanted.

"Osman!" I called frantically for my sleeping wonderguard. It was a marvel how he could sleep through this, I thought, but reconsidered. It was a marvel I was foolish enough to think he would even hear this in his sleep. "Osman!" I shouted. He finally appeared around the corner of the courtyard, with a large stick and larger eyes. He was terrified. "It's only the cat," I muttered to reassure myself more than him. His eyes were glazed with apprehension, but he gave me a reproachful look that said, "See, I told you about having worthless cats." He held his stick in front of his body to defend himself.

"Let's get her into the back room," I said. However whenever I moved toward her, she retreated, wrinkling up her nose and slashing viciously with her claws extended. Osman cowered right behind me, carefully following my every step so as to keep me between him and the cat.

I grabbed the broom from the kitchen in case Malvey lost it entirely and attacked me. I could tell that Osman was not going to relinquish his stick. I told him to go back and close both the door to the bedroom and the door to the main part of the house so she could not run past us and hide. I put some milk into the back room hoping she would want breakfast and follow me quietly. She was determined however, to stay where she was, pacing and howling along the wall of the open courtyard.

"If you opened the outside door I think she would run out," said Osman, hopeful he could get rid of the cat forever.

"This will pass, Osman," I said firmly. "She's just come into heat. It will only last a few days." I was not reassuring him or me. One of the days was my tea party and who knew how long wild cats stayed in heat.

I was startled by a shower of little rocks and dust falling from the top of the courtyard wall as a wild male cat jumped on top of it. He crouched there, realizing if he jumped down into the little bordello he would be trapped. Despite the certain danger below, he was terribly enticed by that little whore, Malvey. She was screaming for sex and sticking her rotating bottom up into the air. Finally Osman had an unprotected target upon which to take out his anger at the little white trouble maker. He picked up pots and cans from the kitchen and threw them at the male cat with deadly aim. The shower of clattering spoons and pot lids frightened Malvey. She ran into the back room and under the bed. I shut the door against the intensity of unrestrained sexual yearning and went back to bed alone.

I left the provocative puss locked up the next day while I finished my party preparations. As I put the finishing touches on the buffet table in my living room, I listened for her. You could hardly hear her howling with all of the doors closed I noted with satisfaction. I had chocolate cookies, chocolate cake with chocolate frosting, and lovely yellow American cheese. There were bottles of orange squash, lemon squash, and lime mixer for drinks. Asha had helped me to make proper spice tea with cardamom and milk. I had cut a checkered cloth into pieces for napkins. It was a feast I thought, sampling yet another piece of the golden cheese. I supposed it wasn't actually good cheese, but it was delicious to someone who had not tasted any for eleven months. We had a little rule among the Somali ex-patriot community. All talk about food was expressly forbidden. You would only make yourself unhappy thinking about juicy hamburgers with french fries dripping with catsup, doughnuts, apple pie, ice cream, jello or coconut cream pie.

Asha and Assia arrived looking like Greek goddesses with the shoulders of their flowing dresses tied up with ribbons. These two women were not only beautiful, they moved with such grace and spirit they embodied everything I believe is feminine. I was mixing orange squash for Asha, when I heard a terrific clatter in the courtyard. I asked Assia to greet any other guests who arrived, and went to see what was the matter. Three male cats, from God knows where, had perched themselves on the top of the courtyard wall. They looked dangerously close to jumping down as I entered. I drove them off with a few badly aimed pots. They jumped down outside, but I was apprehensive about how long they were going to stay down. I called Osman away from fanning the fire for the tea in the back cooking shed and told him to go outside and chase the horny male cats far away.

I was surprised to hear the gay chatter of many voices in my sitting room when I returned. I had worried over making proper introductions, how my guests would get along, and what they would find in common to talk about. I realized that my apprehension had been quite unfounded as I entered the room. There was a lively warm conversation taking place. It was readily apparent that the Somali women all knew each other quite well. Everyone was speaking in English for the benefit of the consul's wife, Susan. "I didn't know you all knew each other," I said in surprise at the evident closeness of the group.

"Of course we all know each other, everyone but Asha went to the same school, the Burao Girls Secondary School," said Halimo, flashing her lovely smile. "We all had the same teacher, Miss Amanda Bell," she told me, and every one of the Somali women smiled and nodded at the mention of her name.

"Tell me about Miss Amanda," asked Susan. She had soft brown hair, a pleasant face and eyes that betrayed wisdom, not pretense. She was a jolly, motherly type, alert and obviously interested in every nuance of my special friends. I was proud that she would represent American women in Somalia.

"She was an older British lady," said Assia.

"She was very strict, and would not allow any non-sense. She shouted if you put your veil over your head to hide from her questions," added Halimo, smiling at the memory.

"We worked so very hard for this woman." Ibado tossed her head up and laughed. "I remember poring over books and compositions as if they were the most important things in the world. She didn't allow us to believe that we would just get married and men would take care of us for the rest of our lives."

"She insisted that we were just as intelligent as the boys. She felt that we had to be the ones to make sensible changes in our country for women and children. She would say, 'If you girls don't do it, no one will,' and we believed her," said Halimo. She was living this challenge in her work at the Hargeisa hospital.

"She was tough, nobody pushed her around. She stood up to the other male teachers and the headmaster. She made sure that we got as much as the boy's school," remembered Amina Nur. Amina wasn't pushed around by the doctors or the male patients at the hospital any more than Halimo was. I had seen her walk right into a vicious fight between two members of different tribes and insist that they stop hitting each other. She made them agree to leave each other alone while they were on the hospital grounds.

Inter-tribal fighting was a constant problem at the hospital since the relatives of the patients came to cook, bathe, and tend the sick person. Camels are not ridden by Somali people, as a rule, but the very ill are carried on a camel's back. Often there were twenty camels on the hospital grounds from different clans and tribes. Each family wanted to set up makeshift living quarters in the tiny spaces outside the patients' rooms. The patients were put into long, low buildings, divided into five or six rooms. There were several such buildings and a large dispensary in the compound that made up the hospital grounds. Space was a constant problem. The families started cooking fires, pilfered water and charcoal, and were quite difficult to control. They were stressed due to the severe illness of their loved one and were not used to being told what to do. Fights erupted daily on the hospital grounds. Dealing with inter-tribal hostilities had not been a topic in the British medical school Amina and Halimo attended, yet this was crucial to the smooth operation of the Hargeisa hospital. Amina and Halimo knew that to send the patient's families away would not be acceptable nor would it hasten the recovery of the sick person. The patients in the hospital did not have modern medicine all the time, but they had the love and constant concern of those who loved them. Who is to say which is a greater help in healing? Amina and Halimo were bridging the gap between modern medical practice and ancient traditions. They fought the doctors, then they fought the nomads. They usually won because they talked sense in both the Somali world and the modern world.

Muslima was deeply committed to the education of women. She came from a wealthy family and certainly did not need to work. She taught in order to pass on the benefit of her own education to young girls. She was tireless and often used her own resources to provide materials for the girl's school in Hargeisa. It was always allotted less resources than the boy's school.

I was stunned. I wondered if Miss Amanda Bell knew the remarkable legacy she had given to the young girls she had taught in Burao. The room was full of thoughtful, elegant, and powerful Somali women. Each one was working against incredible odds of tradition, prejudice, and just plain ignorant fear. Each one was standing up to the powerful forces trying to keep them from making changes to a way of life that had to change.

I was so moved by the immeasurable effect a teacher can have on the lives of students, that I was caught off guard by the prerogative of nature. If I had known what was about to happen, I might have averted a disaster by simply closing a door. But that is the trouble with trouble, we don't think of the obvious solution until later.

I heard the undertones of yowling from the back of the house suddenly escalate to a feverish pitch and hurried

out to see what was going on. Two male cats had reckless-
ly jumped down into the courtyard. They stopped cater-
wauling for a moment in order to decide how much of a
threat I was going to be. Osman, who was standing by the
back door, appeared frozen with fear. When Malvey saun-
tered by however, the cats threw caution to the winds, and
ran after her. She sprinted in circles around the walled
enclosure, stopping occasionally to undulate her behind,
then to hiss and claw at her ardent pursuers. I snatched the
broom and began to flail helplessly at the dervish of determined cats. Hell hath no fury like a pack of mating wildcats
trapped in a small courtyard with an exasperated woman.

Suddenly my little kitty saw an opening and ran
straight for the living room door. I had left it open in my
haste to see what was causing the commotion. She raced
into the room, followed by an impassioned suitor who was
close at her enticing backside. She leaped upon my buffet
table, and in the midst of the chocolate cookies, the chocolate cake, the yellow cheese, and the upturned bottles of
orange squash, was caught by the lecherous male.

He could stand her teasing no more and obeyed the
unsubtle pressure of his male instinct, oblivious to the reality of the situation. He caught her with a roughness that
made kitty cry out, but the cries quickly changed into a
long series of sobs as she pleaded with him to help her. She
writhed and twisted her way toward the summit of ecstacy.
When she squirmed in desperation, trying to impale herself
on the spear of his manhood, her partner shifted position
slightly and mated her right in the middle of my tea table
between the chocolate cake and the orange squash bottle.

He did not have at her long before the other cat, not to
be denied, threw caution to the winds and jumped on the
two of them. Their coitus interruptus was also the interruptus of my tea party. I stood helpless, afraid of the carnal
frenzy, not knowing what to do.

Asha, God bless that woman, quickly opened the front
door and took the broom from my trembling hands. A firm
but directive shove was all that was needed. She always did
have the light touch. She did not frighten the cats any fur-

ther, but opened their eyes to an avenue of escape. They all ran outside to freedom and the open desert where they could mate in private, witnessed only by Allah the Merciful.

Susan showed true diplomatic aplomb, and burst out laughing gaily. Her jolly spirit was infectious and we all joined the emotional relief. "I just love this place," said Susan. "I've been trapped with diplomats in Europe for the last few years. There is such a special energy here, I feel close to life itself."

The wreckage on the table was ignored as a very special bond was forged among the women in my living room. They were not satisfied by the dainty crumbs tradition allocated to the female sex, but by the hearty bonds of friendship and the challenges of a life full of passion.

My wretched cat came back a few days later, exhausted. She ate everything I fed her, then lay on her special pillow with a contented sigh, and turned back into my cuddly kitty.

I never did figure out how she escaped from the back room, unless Osman opened the door in an attempt to get rid of her for once and for all. Most of the time Malvey lived in a sheltered world of comfortable amenities, but when necessary, she returned to more ancient traditions which transcend time and progress. Halimo arranged for one of the British nurses at the hospital to take her when I left to go back to the States. She sent me pictures of kitty's first litter. It was a mixture of grey and yellow striped kittens but one had black rings around the tail. I can only hope that kitty also inherited the wonderful wild streak of its mother. She was a determined female, that cat; when she saw what she wanted she found a way to get it.

I hope that my beautiful friends held on to their determination to get what they wanted for the women of their country and that someday they will be successful. I don't know because I never saw them again, and I fear that I never will.

The
Last Day

The
Last Day

Be they Muslims, Jews
Christians or Sabians
those who believe in God
and the Last Day
and who do good
have their reward with
the Lord
They have nothing to fear,
and they will not sorrow.

—Sura 62, The Cow

I carefully peeled the white paper backing from the precious bit of tin foil on the gum wrapper and smoothed it out on my wooden table. I chewed this one last piece of gum while I retrieved my little pile of tin foil wrappers from the box where I had been storing them. It was another bright beautiful morning, a few days before Christmas, 1969. I selected the smallest of the wooden camel bells I had purchased for outrageous prices from Osman Tuuk, and painstakingly pasted the scraps of tin foil on the bell. Yes! I would have Christmas decorations.

I anticipated everyone's delighted surprise at my silvery Christmas bells. I also had a secret cache of chocolate and had asked Osman to spend the following afternoon fanning my charcoal stove so that I could bake a chocolate cake. The chocolate would cover up the weevil flavor in the flour, and my mouth watered at the thought of the sweet dark cake after Christmas dinner.

I was surprised to hear the whir of tires driving up the side of the rocky hill to my house and screech to a stop in front of my door. The pace of life in Somalia was hardly ever fast, it was often unusual, but nothing ever hurried. Even before I could unbolt the door, Jack, the American consular, was standing on my steps, next to Osman's dreadful little guard shack.

"Hey, wait a minute," I said because Jack stepped right into the room before I could even say hello. I scurried to hide the Christmas presents I had made for him and Susan, his wife. They were not wrapped and I didn't want to ruin the surprise. "Now don't look!" I said.

"Don't break my heart," he replied ominously and the room was suddenly filled with a disturbing silence.

"What's the matter?" I asked, abruptly aware of his anxious face and nervous body language.

"I want you to come with me to the American compound right now. Get some things, you will be spending the night with us."

"What's going on," I repeated, incredulous.

"Jeanne, the Somali government has ordered all Peace Corps volunteers to leave the country within twenty-four hours. You may be in some danger here alone, and I am taking you to the consulate."

"What," I stammered, my mouth suddenly dry.

"We have arranged for a plane to fly you out of here tomorrow."

I just stood there with my mouth hanging open, my eyes couldn't see for a moment because my brain refused to assimilate this information. I couldn't believe it. This was my home, I had school papers to correct, we were having a test on Thursday, I had a meeting of my girl scout troop on

Saturday. I had been saving tin foil for Christmas since March.

"Hurry," he said. "I have to get back to the consulate." I gathered up a few personal items, and left the shining camel bell hidden because I was sure that things would sort themselves out. This had to be a mistake, a false alarm. Why would the Peace Corps volunteers be ordered to leave the country? What could possibly warrant that?

We drove to the consulate in Hargeisa where several other frightened Peace Corps Volunteers had already gathered. We met together in Jack's office and he explained all that he knew, exactly what he had told me. Suddenly the telephone rang. Everyone held their breath. Jack grabbed the phone mid-ring. He listened, then paused for a moment. I bit my bottom lip. This could not be good news. Finally he said, very slowly, "Hajji, it's for you."

Hajji Mohammed, the Somali administrative assistant, took the receiver and answered the caller in Somali.

"Yes, Yes, *hiyea*, okay," he said to the voice on the line. We waited, anxiously praying for good news. Finally Hajji agreed again, "Yes tomorrow, two o'clock," and hung up the phone. Everyone stared at him, hearts on hold, waiting for the news. He appeared embarrassed, and hesitated. We expected the worst. Finally he sheepishly explained that he would be meeting a friend to play golf at two the following day. We all stared at each other in disbelief. How could our lives be totally disrupted while it carried on as usual for others. I hadn't known there was a golf course in Somalia. "We don't have the grass," explained Hajji earnestly, "just the holes."

Little by little over the course of the afternoon, the story was pieced together. Siad Barre had declared himself a military dictator after the democratically elected President had been assassinated a few weeks ago. For some reason he had demanded the United States Peace Corps withdraw immediately. Radio Hargeisa was saying that Peace Corps volunteers were teaching homosexuality in the schools. The consular was fearful of angry reprisals if the volunteers went into town or back to their homes.

I felt as if a book had been closed right in the middle of the story, as if I had been locked out of my house and there was no way to ever open the door again. I cried when Halimo and Assia came to see me that night. They had heard I was staying at the consulate and came with other friends to say goodby. They accepted this turn of events as the will of Allah; I was angry and afraid. Subti and Abdul Kader came long after dark, cloaked from head to toe in their long *goas* so that no one would recognize them. They were fearful of reprisals for being friends with the Americans. Abdillahi had refused to come with them. I told them to meet me at my house in the morning and I would give them all of my books for the school and let them take whatever else they wanted. Abdul Kader said he knew someone with a truck they could borrow to bring the books over to the school. I watched them walk away into the darkness of the black Somali night for the last time.

Asha came with her sisters and we hugged and cried. I gave her my head scarves, I would not need them anymore to cover my head from Allah.

Ali Esa drove me back up to my house before dawn the next day. It seemed so strange not to watch the light move across my bedroom in the morning, not to go to school. It was odd to arrive at my house in a car. Ali Abdi stood in the shadows shyly waiting when we got out of the Land Rover. He gave me a colorful hand-beaded spear and explained that his sister had made it. He wanted me to write to him and said that he hoped to come and study in the United States someday. I hoped that he would.

I paced around the living room and did not know where to begin. I didn't want to leave. How could I possibly pack in a few hours? What was important?

Suddenly I heard voices outside and opened the door expecting more friends had come to say goodby. Instead I was stunned to see a large crowd of people I did not know. They pushed right by me into my own home. The men and several brazen women began to pick up my possessions and carried whatever they wanted out the door. I couldn't believe it. I shouted and screamed, but Ali Esa quickly pulled me into a corner and whispered that I should stop it immediately. He was right, the men were acting ugly and taunted me to my face. It would not have taken much to start a fist fight. They made comments about the white devil whore and picked through my dishes, cosmetics, and even my underwear while I stood helplessly watching. I felt as if I did not exist. I bit my lips so hard they bled and stood there in a white rage daring them to touch me. I am sure that only Ali Esa, tall and composed, kept them away from me. They had been told that the Peace Corps teachers were infidels on the radio and that we were undermining the practice of Islam.

I heard a car outside and was relieved to see Abdul Kader and Subti arrive with some other friends. They shouted and kicked at the intruders, claiming that these things belonged to them and these people were stealing from them, not the infidel white. I was glad I had given my books to my friends the night before. The intruders left jeering at me as they passed and Ali told me to pack what I wanted to take as fast as I could. He was afraid the mob would return with others and something dangerous might develop.

To my immense relief, no one had touched the precious things I wanted to take home with me. My camel bells, the sandals Osman sold me one at a time, the Shifta hat, my *goa,* my Somali dresses and slips, and my milk baskets had been ignored. These ordinary things were of little interest to the Somalis who came to loot. Only the worn out Western things had been taken. My faded and stiff dresses (the house girl never rinsed them, she only soaped) were gone, my guitar with only two strings left, my hairbrush, my clock, the flashlight Abdillahi didn't want because it didn't work, and my radio had been stolen.

Now that did make me mad. I intended to give that radio to Osman Tuuk since he was the one who listened to it most of the time. I would have nothing but money to give my faithful tormentor.

Amina entered by the back door, as always, elegant, composed, and alert. My dear friend I thought. How I would miss her, the smell of spice tea, the swish of her skirts, her gentle hennaed hands. She was shouting and throwing rocks at the remnants of the crowd still hovering outside my door. "Those stupid nomads!" she exclaimed, obviously embarrassed by their actions. She went on about how terrible these people were acting, then appeared totally exasperated as she told me that she had seen Osman taking my radio home with him.

"Well, it was sort of his radio," I explained, but half-heartedly. I felt worse about Osman taking the radio than the people who had robbed my house in front of my eyes.

Amina gave me two beautifully woven baskets made of reeds she had gathered and dyed with natural colors. She proudly pointed out the hot pink plastic edging she had sewn around the lip of each basket. At first I had thought I would remove the plastic bands because they ruined the natural look of the baskets; but I never did because they were gifts from my beloved neighbor and I wouldn't change a thing that she had touched.

Ali was loading my trunk into the back of the Land Rover when Osman appeared. "Osman," I said, looking right into his eyes. "You did not have to steal the radio, I was going to give it to you."

He met my gaze right on and denied stealing it. I knew by the puzzled look in his eyes that he had taken the radio because he considered it his, and how could he steal what already belonged to him? How could I give him something he already owned? Why was I angry at him about his radio? I sighed and considered again how I simply could not understand gifts in Somali terms. To the Somali everything belongs to Allah. I gave Osman his pay for the next few months. I wondered how he would survive if there were no foreigners to sell things to, no one to guard. I hoped he would not be in trouble because he had worked for the Americans.

Ali was in a terrific hurry. He would not allow any lingering goodbys. I shouted at Amina to have the kitchen things and my hot water bottle for her mother, Howa, but I don't know if she heard me because Ali was roaring down the hill.

Late that afternoon, we formed a convoy of three Land Rovers at the Consulate compound to drive out to the Hargeisa airport. Miraculously all of the volunteers in the Northern Region had been found and were ready for the flight out of the country. I sat in the front car next to the volunteer who was driving, Steve. He was joking and trying to cheer me up. I couldn't stop the tears rolling down my face. This was my home, I wasn't ready to leave. I couldn't stop crying. My tears were replaced by terror when we were stopped by an armed roadblock just outside of town.

Four men with rifles stood across the road and a fifth approached the car when we stopped. He looked younger than most of my students, and I could see that he had no idea what he was supposed to be doing in his shabby shirt and ma'awiess. I was afraid of his fear. He asked Steve if he had a driver's license in Somali. I understood some of his discomfort since regular police were required to speak English. I translated and Steve handed over his Somali driver's license. Much to our shock he tore up the paper and said, "Now, you do not have a license to drive the car." I realized he was making an attempt to get himself a car. He thought if Steve could not legally drive we would have to abandon the car.

Furious at this stupid little trick, I fished in my purse. "I have a license," I said in Somali, staring defiantly right into his eyes. Women in Muslim countries did not drive, did not look men in the eyes, and white women did not speak Somali. He was obviously shocked and stepped back from the car. Steve got out and went around to the other side, the men in front of the car moved away and I put the idling motor into first gear.

That's when he reached into the open window and jammed the barrel of his gun into my mouth. I went limp and lost control of my bodily functions. I felt hot urine spill unrestrained down my legs and drip into the shoe still holding down the clutch. There were no seconds because there was no breathing and there were no thoughts because there was no time.

The gunman turned at the sound of a car coming from

the other direction and slowly pulled the gun barrel out of my mouth. An officer in uniform jumped out. He signaled that we should pass. I could taste the metal of the gun barrel the rest of the way to the airport.

Jack had to carry me onto the plane because I couldn't feel my legs. I ceased to function physically; I was totally overwhelmed with the events of my last hours in Northern Somalia. I was overwhelmed by the depth of the friendship and love I felt from my friends and by the depth of the hatred I felt from strangers who judged me by the color of my skin, my religion, my country.

Living in Somalia was like somehow actually going back in time and living there. However, just as the last camel in line walks as quickly as the first, events in advanced nations have an impact on the least of the nations, even the astrophysical discovery of black holes. Just when you feel that time stands still in Somalia because it is rooted in the sway of the camels' endless parade across the desert, you fall into a black hole and nothing is ever the same again.

Epilogue

In January 1989, government soldiers, under the direction of Siad Barre, the military dictator, swept through the Northern Region of Somalia. They blew up all of the buildings in Arabsiyo, poisoned the wells, destroyed the orchards, and killed many of the inhabitants. They buried land mines throughout the area. Like the tenacious desert, the villagers slowly returned, but life will never be simple in Arabsiyo again.

I wrote this book to record the history of this little village.

— Jeanne D'Haem
February 21, 1997